From Footers
To
Finish Nails

Dr. Bo Wagner

FROM FOOTERS
TO
FINISH NAILS

Word of His Mouth Publishers
Mooresboro, NC

All Scripture quotations are taken from the **King James Version** of the Bible.

Some names have been changed to protect the identity of these individuals.

Cover Art by Chip Nuhrah

ISBN: 978-0615489544
Printed in the United States of America
© 2008 Dr. Bo Wagner (Robert Arthur Wagner)

Word of His Mouth Publishers
PO Box 256
Mooresboro, NC 28114

PREFACE

The call was unexpected. I recognized the name and the voice of the gentleman I went to Bible College with several years previous, but whom I knew only in passing. He asked if he could come see me right away, and I told him he could.

When he arrived, there was an awkward moment of silence, as he just stared at me. Finally he said, "I don't know why I'm here, I don't even like you!" Laughing, I told him he would have to stand in line behind a bunch of others who had already arrived at that place.

Finally, the floodgates broke. He began to cry, and unfolded the story of how his wife had left him, and no one at the school, or his church, had any interest of helping. Thus began the process of restoring a home that was in ruins. It took several months, lots of prayer, and the grace of God above all else, but as of this writing, they are still together, doing well, and are in the ministry serving God faithfully.

The story of troubles like that are by no means uncommon, nor are accounts of God's power to restore broken homes.

But why, I wonder, does it even need to reach that point? We have the inspired word of God, which is loaded with instructions on the building and maintaining of a home. Would it not be much better to start it right, run it right, and make it from day one what God would have it to be, than to try and fix it after the damage is done?

Our church recently built a new, 11,000 square foot building from the ground up. During that process, God impressed upon my heart how much building a building is like building a home. That began a series of messages in my church. I am honored to present it to you now, in book form, with the prayer that it will make a difference.

Dr. Bo Wagner, October 28, 2008

Table of Content

Chapter	Title	Page
	Introduction	11
1	Site Preparation	13
2	Digging the Footers	27
3	The Septic System	39
4	Keeping the Workers From Killing Each Other	47
5	Eliminating Enemies From Below	63
6	Anchor Bolts	75
7	Bringing the Main Beams Together	87
8	Preparing for a Rainy Day	99
9	"I" is for Insulation	111
10	Sure I Have a Security System: That Screen Door is Top of the Line	115
11	Windows, Wonderful Windows	131
12	Framed for Success or Framed for Failure	147
13	Six Strand and Cat Five	157
14	O Lord, Send the High Voltage, 3 Phase, 600 Amp Power Just Now	171
15	1400 Reason I Can No Longer See Through Walls	179
16	HVAC: Tons of Correction, Pleasant Results	191
17	Everything You Need to See Is Under the Ceiling	203
18	Just to Make it Nice	209
	Endnotes	221
	Epilogue	223

INTRODUCTION

Proverbs 16:9 A man's heart deviseth his way: but the LORD directeth his steps.

      This is our foundational verse for this book. It means that people decide how they want things to be; for instance they decide that they want a good home, a home that will be loving and stable and will not have to go through divorce or be hate-filled and miserable. They decide these things, they devise ways to make it happen, but it is only the LORD that can direct our steps to get that job done.

      Men and women and boys and girls are very good at devising, but not so good at being directed. That is why so many of the good things they devise end up falling through!

      If our homes are going to be what they should be, if they are going to avoid divorce and be sweet and pleasant and have good parent/child relationships, they are going to have to be directed by God's Word.

      Most of my church knows a thing or two about construction. Many of us know *a lot* about construction, especially those of us who have been building the new church building. I myself have roughly 16,000 hours of labor invested in it. We have seen this building go from non-existent to almost done. We have gotten our hands dirty and our brows sweaty.

Building a home, I have found, is a lot like building a building. You don't start from the roof, then pour the foundation, then lay carpet, then put up beams, then hang lights, then dig footers. You just don't. There is an order in which things need to be done. Likewise, it's awfully helpful to start from the beginning and work our way upward in order to get our homes built right. For that reason, I named this book on the home *From Footers To Finish Nails.* Since the material herein came from a series of messages I preached, please give me some mercy when you consider it's grammatical construction. At times while reading it, you will be able to tell very clearly that what you are reading was preached first, and then transferred to book form. You may feel as if you are in the pew while taking it all in, and that is fine with me. This book is not designed to be an example of great literary form and prowess; it is intended to help people build their homes in a Biblical manner. Thank you for reading it, and I hope it is a blessing!

Dr. Bo Wagner, November 24, 2008

PART ONE:
SITE PREPARATION

Once upon a time, in a little country community, there was a nice little fishing pond. It was fed by five natural springs, and never once went dry. Through the years, the people in the community would come and fish in that little pond. They would spend their days snagging buckets of bream, and every now and then a 20 or 30 pound catfish!

But time marches on, and a community marches right along with it. One day, the owner of that little fishing pond that everyone loved so well decided that the fishing pond wasn't needed anymore. So he filled in the pond, and put in underground drains to try and divert the natural springs. And then, where the fishing pond had once been, he built a little concrete block building. That building became a restaurant, and people far and wide came to eat where the little pond had once been.

But the little pond wasn't so easy to get rid of. For starters, the building that sat where the little pond had once been was still the lowest spot in the entire town. And as more and more people came to the little community, the dirt road was paved, driveways were poured, and since the rain water had little ground to sink into anymore, all of the water in town ran to that one little spot where the restaurant sat, where the little fishing pond once had been. To make matters more complicated, the old pipes used to divert the natural springs broke down over time, and often flooded the yard of the little restaurant. When it rained, things were even worse, with the entire floor of the restaurant often flooding.

And then one day, some people who didn't know any of this, put a church in that little former restaurant. And forever after the pastor wished a plague on the rotten so-and-so who decided to build a building on top of a fishing pond...

I'm sure you recognize that as the story of our church. Now, I'm kidding about the plague part. The truth is, I'm glad that the old building was here for us to buy and start a church in. But there is no denying the fact that the sight preparation that went into building this building was a disaster! If you tried to build another building on this spot today, the EPA and OSHA and the Cleveland County Building Inspectors and the FBI and the CIA and Al Qaeda and the boy scouts would all have you shot. This was a terrible piece of ground to build a building on, and because of that, we are still having trouble with water to this very day! Good sight preparation is essential to good building.

Good site preparation is also essential to building a good home. You need to decide where you are going to build your family! Let's delve into that thought from Scripture. As we do, understand that the first couple of chapters from this book will be very basic. You may not read anything you did not already know, but I assure you that you will read things that are essential nonetheless. As the book progresses, there will be many things much more in depth, but as with any foundation, the beginning must needs be basic.

Your home needs to be built at Calvary.

I am speaking of personal salvation here. Yes, it is true that we are forbidden to marry an unsaved person (II Cor. 6:14) and we will deal with that in the next chapter. But I want to deal in this chapter with the fact that if your home is ever going to be what it should be you need to be saved.

This is, quite simply, step one. It is the first thing you need to make sure of. Many times I have had people come to me for marriage counseling, people who have been referred to me by someone. A lot of those times, it is quickly evident that I can give all of the Biblical counsel I want and it is not going to help, because I am trying to counsel lost people, and lost people don't have the capacity to grasp and then internalize the word of God. Here is why I say that:

I Corinthians 2:14 *But the natural man receiveth not the things of the Spirit of God: for they are foolishness unto him: neither can he know them, because they are spiritually discerned.*

I can explain faithfulness, and fidelity, and sacrificial love, and the necessity of keeping vows to a lost person all I want, and they just aren't going to "get it" like they should, because those things from God's Word are spiritually discerned, and they don't have the Holy Spirit to help them discern those truths.

There is probably someone reading this right now who really wants your marriage to be better, and it just isn't going to get any better because you are lost. Dr. Wagner cannot help you, Dr. Phil cannot help you, Oprah cannot help you, Dr. Ruth cannot help you. It's going to take the blood of Jesus applied to your heart and the Holy Ghost of God indwelling you for things in your home to ever get better.

I am probably writing to some right now who are single, and looking forward to getting married some day, and you really want to have an awesome, fulfilling marriage; and the truth of the matter is that it isn't going to happen unless you get saved first.

Marriage was invented by God: **Genesis 2:18** *And the LORD God said, It is not good that the man should be alone; I will make him an help meet for him. 19 And out of the ground the LORD God formed every beast of the field, and every fowl of the air; and brought them unto Adam to see what he would call them: and whatsoever Adam called every living creature, that was the name thereof. 20 And Adam* *gave names to all cattle, and to the fowl of the air, and to every beast of the field; but for Adam there was not found an help meet for him. 21 And the LORD God caused a deep sleep to fall upon Adam, and he slept: and he took one of his ribs, and closed up the flesh instead thereof; 22 And the rib, which the LORD God had taken from man, made he a woman, and brought her unto the man. 23 And Adam said, This is now bone of my bones, and flesh of my flesh: she shall be called Woman, because she was taken out of Man. 24 Therefore shall a man leave his father and his mother, and shall cleave unto his wife: and they shall be one flesh.*

God did this. He invented marriage. And the God, who invented marriage, wants to be at the center of every marriage. You may be wealthy, or smart, or attractive. You may have those things to bring into your marriage. But if you don't have the Lord Jesus Christ to bring into your marriage, you're missing the one thing that can hold it all together and make it heaven on earth!

Before we started building the new building, we had to clear an old building off of the site. That old "Country Coliseum" had to go. It was a burned out hulk, ugly and dangerous. Sir, Ma'am, that is exactly what you face when you try to build a home without being saved. You have a dangerous, ugly hulk of sin on the sight where you intend to build. You're not going to build anything new that way, you're just going to add onto what needs to be torn down to start with, and it will be even more dangerous and more ugly than it was before. You need a fresh start; you need to build your home at Calvary.

Your home needs to be built at the local church.

Psalm 84:1 *How amiable are thy tabernacles, O LORD of hosts! 2 My soul longeth, yea, even fainteth for the courts of the LORD: my heart and my flesh crieth out for the living God. 3 Yea, the sparrow hath found an house, and the swallow a nest for herself, where she may lay her young, even thine altars, O LORD of hosts, my King, and my God.*

16

This is a beautiful passage. It is the only time that the word "amiable" appears in the Bible. That word means "utterly beautiful." And here is an amazing thing to realize about this: David wrote this Psalm to Asaph when he was driven out of the kingdom by Absalom. This was well before Solomon took the throne, well before the magnificent temple was built. David thought that the house of God was beautiful when the house of God was little more than a tent!

I rejoice that we are building a new building, but as far as I'm concerned, the one we're still in is beautiful to me as well. We've been meeting with God here.

But here is the part of this passage I really love; verse three: **Psalm 84:3** *Yea, the sparrow hath found an house, and the swallow a nest for herself, where she may lay her young, even thine altars, O LORD of hosts, my King, and my God.*

In David's day, birds had made their way into the house of God and made nests there, and they were raising their babies there.

I wonder who noticed that first? I can almost imagine some priest wandering into the house of God, and seeing that nest, and hearing the chirping. I can almost see him blowing a gasket at the "irreverence" of those fowl. I have in my mind that he was moving towards those nests, ready to dispose of them, when he heard the voice of king David call out from behind him "Stop! If those birds have enough sense to raise their babies in the house of God, let them alone. They have more sense than a lot of people I know."

There is no way to overestimate how important it is to build your home at the house of God. Before you ever get married, you need to be in the habit of coming to God's house for Sunday school, Sunday Worship, Sunday night, Wednesday night, and revival. Sunday school, Sunday Worship, Sunday night, Wednesday night, and revival. Sunday school, Sunday Worship, Sunday night, Wednesday night, and revival.

Unless you are sick, or working your regular job, you should be in God's house for Sunday School, Sunday Worship, Sunday Night, Wednesday night, and revival.

17

This church is pretty good at this, and I am grateful, but it could still be better. I love all of you, I have nothing against any of you, I just want what's best for you. If I didn't think it was best for you to be here for Sunday school, Sunday Worship, Sunday Night, Wednesday night, and revival, then I wouldn't be here myself during those times.

Before I ever became a pastor, I was faithful to the house of God for Sunday school, Sunday Worship, Sunday Night, Wednesday night, and revival. And I can tell you that most of the things I learned that have helped to make me a good husband were things I learned in services other than the Sunday morning service! I learned a really great lesson on the home from a Sunday night message on eagles. God squeezed my heart about loving Him and my family and others far more than myself during a song sung during a Wednesday night service. I learned an incredible lesson on discernment that helps me to this day with my children, and I learned it at the end of a Sunday night service.

I do not believe in being harsh and mean like some preachers. I have literally heard preachers say "Hey you buzzards! If you don't come to Sunday night and Wednesday night services, then just go somewhere else. We want faithful people here." That is not just harsh and mean, it is also pretty stupid. I would rather a person come one time a week to services here instead of no times a week to services here. I'm going to love you just as much and treat you just as well whether you come to every service every week or just one of them. But I can promise you certain things if you do choose to be faithful for every service.

I can promise that you will be a big blessing to me. I work just as hard on the Sunday night and Wednesday night messages as I do on the one for Sunday morning, and it does my heart good to see that that labor is not in vain, and I am not preaching to half-empty pews.

I can promise you that you and your home will be blessed by coming. The more time you spend in God's house with God's people, the stronger your home will be. I have seen very few homes who were in the house of God for every service ever break up!

Just stop and think of the alternatives; what is there on TV on Sunday night or Wednesday night that is going to help your home more than the preaching at the house of God?

What is there at the ball game on Sunday night or Wednesday night that is going to help your home more than the worshiping at the house of God?

And here is where the devil is so very good at what he does. A couple will begin to have trouble in their marriage or parents will begin to have trouble with their kids, and the first thing the devil does is whisper in their ear "you don't need to go to church, that would be too embarrassing right now." You should have the sense to know that he's not trying to help you by making you think that.

This is foundational stuff. You need to have this down pat before you ever start "hanging pictures on the wall!" Young people, decide right now not to "like" anyone who isn't in the house of God every time the doors are open. If you do, count on things not getting any better once you have married that person.

Your home needs to be built at a home devotion spot.

Deuteronomy 6:5 *And thou shalt love the LORD thy God with all thine heart, and with all thy soul, and with all thy might. 6 And these words, which I command thee this day, shall be in thine heart: 7 And thou shalt teach them diligently unto thy children, and shalt talk of them when thou sittest in thine house, and when thou walkest by the way, and when thou liest down, and when thou risest up. 8 And thou shalt bind them for a sign upon thine hand, and they shall be as frontlets between thine eyes. 9 And thou shalt write them upon the posts of thy house, and on thy gates.*

All of this, the word, prayer, worship, yes it takes place at the house of God, and yes, Hebrews 10:25 commands us to be there for it, but if our devotions are limited to what we get at the house of God, our homes are going to be weak.

Every young person or single person in this church needs to be having regular Bible reading and prayer time at home every single day. If you do this, God will prepare you to be the right kind of husband or wife before you ever walk down that aisle.

Before I ever met Mrs. Dana, I was at home having my private devotions, and I came across I Corinthians 13, the great love chapter. That chapter taught me how I was supposed to act when I did get married. I had heard it preached before, I had read it before, but this time it really got me. I studied every single phrase, learned what it meant, and then prayed for God to make me like that.

Before I ever met Mrs. Dana, my personal devotions led me to the book of Proverbs, where I really was gripped by the fact that I was supposed to be hard working, and wise in how I handled money. That's come in handy a bunch of times in the last 13 years!

Every married person needs to have his or her own time of Bible reading and prayer every day. If you do this, God will use His Word to correct you when you would never listen to another person and let them correct you. Try doing this. Try having regular personal devotions at home, and watch what happens. You and your spouse will get into a fuss, and you'll be so mad you could chew steel beams and spit nails, and then you'll huff off to do you devotions, and it will just happen to be from **Ecclesiastes 7:9** *Be not hasty in thy spirit to be angry: for anger resteth in the bosom of fools.*

Try doing this. Try having regular personal devotions at home, and watch what happens. Your kids will be driving you so crazy you'll be just about to give up and feed them to the wolves. You'll slip off somewhere quite and pray, and break open your Bible, and it will fall open to: **Proverbs 22:6** *Train up a child in the way he should go: and when he is old, he will not depart from it.*

Let me insert another quick word to the young people right here; you try doing this, trying having regular personal devotions at home, and watching what happens. You young people will have a battle with mom and dad, and you'll think you have the worst home-life in the world. Then you'll head for your room and have your prayer time, and while you're praying God will bring back to your mind those times when your mom stayed by your bed all night when you were sick, or that time when your dad worked a bunch of overtime to send you somewhere special, and all the sudden your heart will soften and you'll find your bedside wet with tears, because God broke your heart during those precious moments of personal devotion. Next thing you know you'll be hugging up to mom and dad, and the sweetest peace will fill your soul as things are made right. I'm telling you if you want to have a good home life, it's not likely to happen unless you are having personal devotion time.

Every young person or single person needs to be having regular Bible reading and prayer time at home every single day. Every married person needs to have his or her own time of Bible reading and prayer every day.

Every home needs to have family devotions as well. There needs to be a time, every day that you are together, that you have a few minutes of family Bible time and prayer. Now, you who are scared to death at the thought of this, let me help you. This doesn't mean that you have to "preach at home!" We're not talking about a miniature church service here. Family devotions can be as simple as reading a few verses, sharing prayer requests, and then praying. Truthfully, one of the worst things you can do is "sermonize" during family devotions. Don't ever use family devotion time to beat your family with the Bible: *You snotty little punk! You better obey me cause the Bible says you have too! Nya nya nya!*

That's a really great way to make your family hate the Bible forever. Use your family devotion time to draw you family nearer to God, His word, His house, and each other. Use it to make them fall in love with Jesus. If questions come up, answer them if you can. If you can't, write them down and bring them to your pastor. You have to learn somehow, and that is a pretty good way to learn!

Your home needs to be built in the halls of service.

Look at a few verses that help to tell the story of Samuel and his family: **1 Samuel 1:24** *And when she had weaned him, she took him up with her, with three bullocks, and one ephah of flour, and a bottle of wine, and brought him unto the house of the LORD in Shiloh: and the child was young. 25 And they slew a bullock, and brought the child to Eli. 26 And she said, Oh my lord, as thy soul liveth, my lord, I am the woman that stood by thee here, praying unto the LORD. 27 For this child I prayed; and the LORD hath given me my petition which I asked of him: 28 Therefore also I have lent him to the LORD; as long as he liveth he shall be lent to the LORD. And he worshiped the LORD there."*

This was a great family. They served God together, including their young son.

We haven't changed subjects. We're still talking about how to have a good home life. And I'm telling you that one of the surest ways to make that happen is to be a family that serves God together. Here is why this works. Most every problem that people have with each other involves selfishness and self-centeredness. This starts as babies! When kids are fighting over a toy, isn't the problem usually that both kids want the other kids to have that toy, and they just won't be satisfied until they're allowed to give that toy to the other kid instead of keeping it for himself? Not hardly! Selfishness starts good and early in life. Selfishness and self-centeredness are poison to a good home life.

Just stop and think about it. You put two people in a small home. And then two becomes three, and three becomes four. But there are only one or two bathrooms. That never causes any squabbles, now does it?

There is a young husband and young wife. They're just starting out, they both have low-paying jobs, and just a tiny amount of money left over after the bills are paid. She's real sure they need to invest in a used washing machine, since their hand-me-down 35 year old model broke down last month and she's been washing by hand ever since. But he's real sure that they need to spend that money on a nice rifle, in case times ever get tough. You know, that way he could go shoot some rabbits for them to eat. That won't be any kind of problem at all, now will it? So I say again, most every problem that people have with each other involves selfishness and self-centeredness. Self-centeredness causes all kinds of problems. It may cause shouting, or it may go the other way and cause the silent treatment:

A man and his wife had gotten into this self-centeredness for some reason, and were full bore into giving each other the silent treatment. This had lasted for days, and no one said so much as a word. Just glares and grunts. Suddenly, the man realized that he would need his wife to wake him up at 5:00 am for an early morning business flight. But he didn't want to be the first one to speak and break the silence. So he wrote out a note in big bold letters: WAKE ME UP AT 5:00 AM! The next morning, he woke up at 10:30 am. Furious, he was about to give his wife the what-for for not waking him up, until he saw another piece of paper sitting on his chest. That piece of paper said, "IT'S 5:00 AM. WAKE UP!"

I say again, self-centeredness is poison to a good home life. And the easiest way in the world to help eliminate that is be a family that serves, and serves together. Moms and dads, load your kids up as often as you can, take them down to a nursing home, and let them wheel folks around. Let them get to know some of those folks personally, and then pray for their needs together. Let them adopt some of them to bring birthday cards and gifts to, and Christmas as well. Your kids need to have their eyes opened to how good they have it, and adopting some folks at a nursing home will do it. It is really hard to raise a selfish, self-centered kid that way.

Husbands and wives, pick some facet of the ministry to serve in together. Adopt a flower garden out front to weed and tend to. Take it on yourselves to clean up the auditorium after the services. Go to work in the bus ministry. It will be difficult for you to be selfish and self-centered at home once you get into the habit of being some of the first ones up on Sunday morning, heading to the church to crawl on the bus, and driving through the highways and hedges so you can love little boys and girls to Jesus. You mark it down, if you do, you and your wife will find yourself crying over them together, and praying over them together, and the closer you get to them, the closer you'll get to each other.

This is one reason why I am so glad that my wife is right there for about every part of my ministry. We have mopped floors together, and knocked on doors together, and visited hospitals together, and done paperwork together, and the more we have served together, the closer we have grown together.

I couldn't let her go now if I tried. It would take a dumb man to give up a good wife, but it would take a full-blown fool to give up a wife, secretary, piano player, janitor, groundskeeper, botanist, and IT expert all rolled into one!

Husbands and wives, right now in your own minds, ask yourself this question: what are you doing to serve God together? If the answer is "nothing" or "not much," you're not doing your relationship any favors.

By the way, everyone can serve somehow. One of the sweetest couples I ever knew was B.L. Queen and his wife. They were both well up in their eighties, serving God together in the nursing home ministry. And they were absolutely sweet on each other till God called him home.

The Sessions are now up in their 60's, and they are still frisky. They embarrass my wife, but one of the reasons that they are like that is because every day, they serve God together.

You know, single or married, I have had very little trouble out of people who were busy serving God. But those pampered little pets who are always getting others to serve them, I have had more trouble out of people like that through the years than you could imagine.

None of these things are complicated, but all of them are absolutely foundational to having a good home. We'll get into some things you may have never heard of or thought of starting in the very next message. But for now, let's start at the beginning, let's handle the site preparation. You need to build your home at Calvary, you need to build your home at the house of God, you need to build your home at a home devotion spot, and you need to build your home in the halls of service.

PART TWO:
DIGGING THE FOOTERS

We just got back from Charleston. We saw a ton of old, historic homes. They all had names. The Russell House. The Carroll Building. And then there was the beautiful home that was built by a young man named Patrick O' Donnell. You may think it would be called The O' Donnell House, or something like it, but it isn't called anything so grand. Instead, it is to this day called "O' Donnell's Folly." Why? Young Mr. Patrick O' Donnell was engaged to a pretty young lady, who truly wanted to marry him. But Patrick O' Donnell decided that an ordinary home like everyone else had wasn't good enough. He decided that before he could possibly marry his dear fiancé, he needed to build a dream home for her, and she would just have to wait till it was done. It took him five years to build that fabulous home... and by that time his fiancé had married someone else. Those two could have used some good, Biblical counseling on how to build a home.

There are several things I learned as we did the foundation for our new church building. I learned that 98-degree days in mid July are not a good time to do an 80x130 foundation. I learned that when you get an architect involved, they will somehow find a reason why you should put $1000.00 of concrete in a hole... twice. I learned that the wind will start blowing the very moment you get 10,000 square feet of plastic laying on the ground.

But I also learned that if you expect your roof to fit right, your footers have to be right.

This is a bit of a shock to most people. The foundation, footers and the roof don't seem to have anything to do with each other, but trust me, they do! If your foundation is not square, things only get worse as the building itself goes up. And by the time you get to putting the roof on, if the foundation isn't right, you'll find that things are so bad out of square, the roof won't fit right. The earliest thing that you do affects everything else all the way to the very end.

Let me say that again: the earliest thing that you do affects everything else all the way to the very end. Young people, are you listening? Because at this point, I'm not talking about building a building anymore, I'm talking about building a home.

There are certain things I encounter in the ministry that just kill me. One of those things is what so often happens with young people. I watch them make bad decisions as pre-teens, teens, twenty-somethings, and then I have to watch them suffer for the rest of their adult lives for a bad decision they made as a kid. That absolutely kills me.

Young people, you have no clue the amount of power you have right now. Let give you the way that I illustrated that in my church.

The first thing I did was to bring up a 12 year old girl, an 18-year-old girl, and an adult lady. Then a boy, 15, a young man 19, and an adult man. I asked the lady if she would like to be an abused wife with a drunken husband who won't even pay the bills. Obviously, her answer was no. Then I asked if she were that unfortunate wife, would she be a little bit upset if she found out that the 12-year-old girl had caused it? Her answer was "Most definitely yes." Then I showed her how it happened. All three are the same person, Sally. The 12-year-old Sally "messed around" a little bit. Didn't actually have sex, just did some heavy petting and kissing. Well, that caused her to get a reputation with the guys. More guys wanted to mess around, she obliged. But within a few years, the guys were older, and 18-year-old Sally wasn't popular anymore for just messing around, she had to do more. So she went to the prom. Dressed immodestly, danced to the world's music, got some guy all hot and bothered, then went out for a party afterward. At the party, she and her date paired off, she figured she was ready, and that night she gave away her purity. Only thing is, she didn't just give something away, she also got something. What she got was a venereal disease. And after she confided in her best friend, a girl she knew she could trust, it didn't take long for everybody in town to know. Suddenly, no guy wanted anything to do with her. After a few years without so much as a date, she finally met a guy. He wasn't at all what she wanted, but she figured that she didn't have much of a choice. So she settled for him, even though he drank, and couldn't hold down a job. Now she is 40ish, married to a bum who won't work, and gets drunk, and beats her up. Who is responsible for what she is now? Look back to the first of the line. The decisions she made way back there have made her what she is now. Dear Sally, if you could go back in time to right before 12-year-old Sally started messing around, what would you say to her? If you could go back in time to when 18-year-old Sally continued the process, what would you say to her?

By now you know how this works, so let's go to the guys. All of them are the same; we'll call them Bob. Young Bob here was kind of straddling the fence, not really going all out for God. But one day during a church service, he got under conviction, and hit the altar during the invitation. He decided right then and there to go all out for God. He started praying, reading his Bible, and serving. He got rid of all worldly music, stopped hanging out with bad friends. At 19, Bob fell for a girl, hard. But his parents and pastor had some real concerns about it. They just didn't have peace about her. They talked to Bob about it, and at first, he was pretty upset. But when he settled down and thought about it, he knew that his parents and pastor had never steered him wrong. It killed him, but he broke off the relationship. After the tears dried, he went right back to serving God. A few years later, he met a girl that made him, and his parents, and his pastor, really REALLY happy. They got married, had kids, and "lived happily ever after." Who is responsible for what he is now? Look back to the first of the line. The decisions he made way back here have made him what he is now. Bob, if you could go back in time to when 12 and 19-year-old Bob made some really good decisions, what would you say to them?

Oh by the way, one more thing. Sally, what would you say if I told you that God never intended for you to marry the loser drunk you married? In fact, God intended for you to marry Bob here, and you would have if you had made better decisions at 12 and 18. You see, that girl that Bob's parents and pastor were leery of? That was you, because of the loose reputation you had managed to earn. Now how upset are you at 12 and 18 year old you?

So let me drive home this statement again: the earliest thing that you do affects everything else all the way to the very end. You literally have the ability to ruin your life before it even gets started good.

There is a man at the church I grew up in that I have used many times as a sermon illustration. He was really important to me as a teenager. Brother Ben and I talked one time about five years back. He told me about when he himself got married. He and his girl were at the church of their youth. The Pastor saw some things that made him very uncomfortable, so he refused to marry them. They went ahead anyway. Twenty-five years later, just about two years ago, they divorced. It took twenty-five years for the mistake of their youth to catch up with them, but it did catch up with them.

There are parents in my church right now who are going through hell on earth in their home. They are dealing with a drunken spouse, or struggling through a third or fourth marriage, and in every single case, the troubles they are going through now can be traced back to the decisions of their youth. I don't say that to hurt them, I say that because they're going to die if you make the same mistakes they made.

Why do some people end up marrying once and staying married for life, while others go through one or more divorces? Because of the decisions they make while they are young.

Why do some people have successful and fulfilling careers, while others struggle just to hang onto a low-paying, miserable job? Because of the decisions they make while they are young.

Why are some people able to drive nice, reliable cars, and live in middle class homes, while others are constantly broken down on the side of the road in a 25 year old car, and spend their entire lives renting whatever home they can get into? Because of the decisions they make while they are young.

Young person, if you will pay attention to me for the next few minutes, and follow the Biblical counsel I give, I can almost guarantee that you will look back and thank me for the awesome life you are living 30 years from now. But if you ignore good counsel and go your own way, bow up and get rebellious and think that you know more than the Bible and more than God, I can pretty much guarantee you that you will spend a few short years living it up, and then it will all crash down around your ears, and you will spend the rest of your life wishing you had listened.

Here are the decisions that should be the foundations for the rest of your life:

I will accept Christ as my Savior if I have not already done so.

John 10:10 *The thief cometh not, but for to steal, and to kill, and to destroy: I am come that they might have life, and that they might have it more abundantly.*

Christ came not just to save you and take you to heaven. But also to give you a wondrous, abundant life on earth. That includes marriage, which without Christ will never amount to much. Perhaps you have been burdened, knowing that you are lost. The smartest thing you can do right now is contact your pastor, and let him lead you to Christ.

I will stay a virgin till I marry.

Hebrews 13:4 *Marriage is honourable in all, and the bed undefiled: but whoremongers and adulterers God will judge.* One of the surest ways to make your life miserable forever is to give away your virginity pre-marriage.

It's hard to find a good person when you have a bad reputation... or an STD... or a baby on your hands. Before I met and married Dana, I met a girl named Pam. She was very attractive, and showed an interest in developing a relationship with me. As we talked, she mentioned what she was going to be looking for in a mate. Above all, she wanted a guy who was a virgin. I was not interested. She wanted a virgin, and so did I. But I knew by her extensive reputation that she wasn't a virgin, even though I still was.

I realize that the world has declared pre-marital sex to be perfectly acceptable. Unfortunately, God never got that memo. And if He ever did, He would crumple it up and throw it away, and continue to expect everyone to live Biblically, which means retaining your virginity till marriage.

I will never ever touch drugs, alcohol, or pornography, nor will I associate with those who do.

Here is the "not touching it" part: **Romans 6:16** *Know ye not, that to whom ye yield yourselves servants to obey, his servants ye are to whom ye obey; whether of sin unto death, or of obedience unto righteousness?*

Every one of these things, drugs, alcohol, pornography, is a "slave master." You don't control it; it controls you! Not one home has ever been "blessed" by any of these things!

A well-respected young couple I knew had it all. Until the filth of pornography ruined the home that everyone thought would stand forever.

A man that made a profession of faith under my ministry, a man to whom God restored a wife, kids, health, and gave him a new reputation, lost it all to alcohol.

A man born into a home of wealth and privilege, the upper echelons of society, found that being born to privilege could not save his home from the ravaging effects of drugs. These things are so very destructive to a home; they are simply never to be touched.

Here is the "not associating" part: **Psalm 1:1** *Blessed is the man that walketh not in the counsel of the ungodly, nor standeth in the way of sinners, nor sitteth in the seat of the scornful. 2 But his delight is in the law of the LORD; and in his law doth he meditate day and night.*

Associating with people who partake of drugs, alcohol, or pornography, will do many things for you, all of which are negative. It will tempt you to do what they are doing, it will give you their reputation whether you are doing like them or not, and it will imply that you condone their behavior. For anyone to have a good home, therefore, they must never touch drugs or alcohol or pornography, and they must never associate with those that do. I will give a much fuller treatment of these three things in a later chapter.

I will not break the law.

Amazingly, shoplifters have trouble getting parents of good kids to approve of them! Ditto for people who are in gangs, or sell drugs.

Romans 13:1 *Let every soul be subject unto the higher powers. For there is no power but of God: the powers that be are ordained of God. 2 Whosoever therefore resisteth the power, resisteth the ordinance of God: and they that resist shall receive to themselves damnation. 3 For rulers are not a terror to good works, but to the evil. Wilt thou then not be afraid of the power? do that which is good, and thou shalt have praise of the same: 4 For he is the minister of God to thee for good. But if thou do that which is evil, be afraid; for he beareth not the sword in vain: for he is the minister of God, a revenger to execute wrath upon him that doeth evil.*

People with criminal records will struggle to find a good mate, struggle to get a good job, and they struggle to have any form of a marriage survive. A lady came to see my wife and myself some years back, and unfolded for us how her husband was selling drugs. No amount of counseling was able to help, and the home dissolved.

I will handle my money well from my first allowance to my Social Security years.

Proverbs 6:6 *Go to the ant, thou sluggard; consider her ways, and be wise:* **7** *Which having no guide, overseer, or ruler,* **8** *Provideth her meat in the summer, and gathereth her food in the harvest.*

Commonly reported statistics report that money is the main cause of 95% of divorces! From years of counseling, I believe it. I do not ever remember counseling a marriage in trouble that did not have money as at least one of the issues.

We are training my son Caleb while young to handle money well. He automatically puts 10% to tithe, whatever offering he chooses, and 30% to savings. As a father, I can assure you that neither my daughters nor my son will get my blessing to marry someone who is careless with money!

I will finish both high school and college (at least community college), **and I will do excellent at both.**

Proverbs 4:7 *Wisdom is the principal thing; therefore get wisdom: and with all thy getting get understanding.*

There is a way to almost ensure you fail in life: drop out!

Imagine, if you will please, this written marriage proposal from dear little Bubba to sweet Mary:

> *"Mayry, sweet Mayry, woodjew giyuv me yer hayund in mayrij? I aint got much, jest a little 1949 single wide on the backside o' mommer n daddy's propity, but luv will make iyut a home. We kin ride orf inta the sunsayut in my 74 Ford Pinto, and hunnymoown dayuwn iyun Gaffney, South Caraliner. Ayund someday, I may evun go back and finish my skewlin.*

I am just guessing that "sweet Mary," if she has a brain in her head, is going to seek after someone that has already "finished his skewlin."

This matter of an education becomes ever more important as the years pass and the economy changes. There was perhaps a time when a couple could survive, maybe even thrive without having finished school. Those days are gone. Mills are closing, assembly jobs are going overseas, and no-one in years to come is likely to secure any type of a decent job without having finished both high school and at least a technical college, and done well at both.

I will not marry as a teenager.

Genesis 2:22 *And the rib, which the LORD God had taken from* **man**, *made he a* **woman**, *and brought her unto the* **man**. *23 And Adam said, This is now bone of my bones, and flesh of my flesh: she shall be called* **Woman**, *because she was taken out of* **Man**. *24 Therefore shall a* **man** *leave his father and his mother, and shall cleave unto his wife: and they shall be one flesh.*

You can clearly see an emphasis in this passage on adulthood. Marriage is no place to grow up! Statistics bear out that the younger you are when you marry, the more likely you are to have that marriage end in divorce. The very first marriage was a man and a woman, not a boy and a girl! A couple came to me for counseling some years back, with a marriage near the breaking point. Sometimes, it takes a great while to draw the problem out. And then there are the times like this one, where as soon as their posteriors landed on my couch across from my desk, the wife blurted out "I am not his momma! If I knew I was going to have to finish raising him, I wouldn't have married him in the first place!" They had married as teens, and he had still not truly become an adult.

I will not marry anyone that my parents and pastor are not thrilled about.

Proverbs 11:14 *Where no counsel is, the people fall: but in the multitude of counselors there is safety.*

Proverbs 15:22 *Without counsel purposes are disappointed: but in the multitude of counselors they are established.*

Proverbs 24:6 *For by wise counsel thou shalt make thy war: and in multitude of counselors there is safety.*

I can honestly say that my mom, Dana's mom and dad, my pastor, Dana's pastor, were absolutely thrilled about our union. There were no negative votes. In fact, my entire church and Dana's entire church, were also absolutely thrilled about our union. Everybody was on board with it. That kind of let me know I was on the right track!

By myself, no matter how strong my feelings, I could not have known, and here is why:

Proverbs 14:12 *There is a way which seemeth right unto a man, but the end thereof are the ways of death.*

Proverbs 16:25 *There is a way that seemeth right unto a man, but the end thereof are the ways of death.*

There was a man named Luther Ingram who once wrote a song entitled "If loving you is wrong, I don't wanna be right."

If loving you is wrong I don't wanna be right, If being right means being without you, I'd rather live a wrong doing life, Your mama and daddy say it's a shame, It's a downright disgrace, Long as I got you by my side, I don't care what your people say.

That is exactly the attitude that people tend to take, and that is not a way to end up happy! That type of attitude starts in a flame of passion and ends in an explosion that destroys a home.

A pastor friend of mine was arm-twisted into marrying a young couple that he knew shouldn't be married. The family threatened to leave and take a bunch of folks with them if he didn't. So he married them. It took less than two years for it to end, and the family left anyway.

I think of Joe and Susanna, who married against everyone's wishes. She got what she wanted, and it was over in less than three months.

I think of Brian and June. I knew that he had grown up with the welfare mentality. My fear was not so much for them getting divorced, but in her sinking to that level and them staying there. That is exactly what has happened.

By the way, if you marry like this, don't think that your parents and pastor are hoping for it to fail. On the contrary, we will be praying as hard as we can that it makes it. But those prayers will probably not do much good.

I will not backslide on God.

It only takes a short time of backsliding to ruin a life. Ask David. His sin with Bathsheba was not the normal behavior in his life. It was just a short episode of backsliding, but oh, what a high price he paid.

On visitation one day, we met and spoke to a nice young couple, which were new to the area. They professed to be saved, and since we had come calling, they began to attend our church. They had a precious little boy, and the entire family began to grow and thrive tremendously. For months they did well. But then they began to slip. They missed a service here, a service there, and soon we had to go hunting for them. We sat down in the same home we had met them at months before, and warned them of the dangers of backsliding. The husband at that point became very belligerent, and, in so many words, told us to mind our own business.

They never came back. Months later, we heard reports that his wife had taken their son and left. A short time later, one of my church leaders ran into the husband in a local grocery store. The hand that was previously carrying a Bible was now cradling a pack of beer. The arm that his wife once leaned on was wrapped around a filthy magazine. The face that once held a smile was now the open domain of sorrow. One of the easiest ways to destroy your home is to backslide on God.

PART THREE:
THE SEPTIC SYSTEM

Thomas Wheeler, CEO of the Massachusetts Mutual Life Insurance Company, tells this story on himself. He and his wife were driving along an interstate highway when he noticed that their car was low on gas. Wheeler got off the highway at the next exit and soon found a rundown gas station with just one gas pump. He asked the lone attendant to fill the tank and check the oil and then went for a little walk around the station to stretch his legs.

As he was returning to the car, he noticed that the attendant and his wife were engaged in an animated conversation. The conversation stopped as he paid the attendant. But as he was getting back into the car, he saw the attendant wave and heard him say, "It was great talking to you." As they drove out of the station, Wheeler asked his wife if she knew the man. She readily admitted she did. They had gone to high school together and had dated steadily for about a year.

"Boy, were you lucky that I came along," bragged Wheeler. "If you had married him, you'd be the wife of a gas station attendant instead of the wife of a chief executive officer."

"Baby," replied his wife, "if I had married him, he'd be the chief executive officer and you'd be the gas station attendant." Ouch!

Thus far, we have dealt with the site preparation, and poured the foundation and footers for the home. Let's move on to the next part of the structure.

How many people do you think could identify which part of the building this is:

It is a part of the building that no modern structure is allowed to be without.

You won't see it once the building is done.

Very few people have any desire to ever work on it should something go wrong.

If it didn't do its job, everybody in the building could get diseased and die a horrible death, or at least have to always wear a clothespin over their nose.

The answer is, of course, the septic or sewage system. I learned to be prepared for so many ministry-type things when I was in Bible College. I learned to be prepared for unexpected deaths in the church family, financial strains, church-discipline, and so many other things. But it didn't take me very long after starting the church to wonder why no professor ever prepared me for other things:

Like the time we had an evangelist in for a revival. We had the red carpet all rolled out... and then an hour before service someone came to me and said "Preacher, all the toilets are backing up!" A couple of us threw on old clothes, grabbed the shovels, and started flinging dirt. We found the blockage (someone flushed a diaper...) and spent the service outside fixing it while everyone else was inside trying to "hold it."

When we started into building the new church, we intended to do it all ourselves. But when it came time to do the rough-in plumbing for the septic, some of our very well-meaning folks said "preacher, let's hire that done. We can't afford to have that the least bit off." So we did. We paid $6300.00. And it worked out so well! It is the only part of the whole thing that we have failed inspection on. We had to pay an extra $1000.00 to have just the field lines re-done. And then we found out that the stub-outs under the slab in the main bathroom were off a bit... a foot and a half or so. We had to cut the concrete out of the bathroom, re-do it, and then re-pour the concrete. That was an extra $500.00. Oh, and then we found out that our genius plumbers didn't even bother to take into account the height of the current tank, already in the ground, when they stubbed out the main lines. They were 8" too low. That cost us $1000.00 more dollars to fix. So our $6300.00 dollar septic system actually cost us $8800.00, and we ended up re-doing most of it anyway. Friends, I could have made that many mistakes for free and saved us the $8,800.00!

That Septic System truly was, no pun intended, a "pain in the tail."

But there is no way at all to do without one. You will never be given a certificate of occupancy until it is in and right and you wouldn't want to be without a septic system even if you could.

Why is that? I think the answer is pretty obvious. Human waste needs to be forever buried in the ground, not flowing through the building. And that is where I want to jump into the home again. You see, there are certain things in humans that are really nothing more than waste and filth; things that can disease and destroy a home, things that need to be forever disposed of and never allowed to see the light of day. If they are not, then no amount of framing or wiring or shingling can help a home survive. No paintings on the wall or flowers in the yard can make up for human waste running through the bedroom, the living room, and the kitchen.

This chapter in itself could be an entire book. Think of all the things that disease and poison homes, even Christian homes! Not little things, not unnoticeable things, but things that are filthy, and vile, and dangerous. And I don't mean the things that corrupt a home from the outside in, like alcohol or drugs or pornography, I mean the things that corrupt a home from the inside out; sins of attitude and action. I am going to deal with several of them, the ones that I believe God has laid on my heart for this chapter. But you be sensitive to the Holy Spirit, He may just deal with some of your own human waste that I don't mention as we deal with the septic system of the home.

Let me begin by choosing the one that I know best, because of my own home life while growing up.

Uncontrolled tempers are human waste.

Ecclesiastes 7:9 *Be not hasty in thy spirit to be angry: for anger resteth in the bosom of fools.*

Proverbs 22:24 *Make no friendship with an angry man; and with a furious man thou shalt not go:*

Proverbs 29:22 *An angry man stirreth up strife, and a furious man aboundeth in transgression.*

James 1:20 *For the wrath of man worketh not the righteousness of God.*

Many of you know a little bit about how I grew up, but none of you know a lot about it. That's because I don't talk about it much; mostly because of the fact that God has been really good to me, so much so that I prefer to live in the present rather than the past. But also because there wasn't much about it that I even care to remember, at least as far as the few years that there was a "father" in the home. If any home ever grew up with the raw sewage of an uncontrolled temper flowing through the home, it was mine.

I can remember being terrified of my adoptive dad. He was a fairly big man, always with about a week of stubble on his face, and was as explosive and unpredictable as a roadside bomb. Once when I was about 5 or 6, my mom told me to go kiss him good night. He was watching TV, and eating some snack. I came up and kissed him on the cheek, unaware that he still had a bit of something in his jaw. He spun like a cat, and backhanded me across the face. I went completely airborne, over a coffee table.

There were many times he would look at me and say "I owe you one" meaning he was going to lash me with a belt, but he never told me or my mom why or what I had done.

I grew up knowing every cuss word in the book, because he used them all. Screaming was the normal order of the day in our house. I walked on eggshells every single day of my young life.

42

The straw that finally broke the camel's back was when he was screaming obscenities at me in the kitchen. I was 9. He was towering over me, cursing at the top of his lungs, my mom was beside me, I was doing my best to stay perfectly still. Suddenly he screamed "don't you cover your ears when I'm talking to you!" I hadn't. But it didn't matter; his temper wouldn't let him see any thing he didn't want to see. When I looked up, he was swinging at my head, closed fist. He would have killed me with that shot. My mom, all 4'11", stepped between us and took it. Then she screamed for me to run for the neighbor.

That was the home I grew up in. That man left when I was nine. He was the reason I took Martial arts later, earning a black belt. I wanted a chance to kill him with my bare hands should he ever come back.

God had to do a work in my own heart, a work of forgiveness, before I could ever be used by Him.

But my point at this moment is to show what absolute sewage an uncontrolled temper is. I don't need any sympathy, God has taken excellent care of me, my life is incredible and fulfilling, I never even think about those days unless I am preaching and they serve as an appropriate illustration. If I saw him today, and he minded his manners, I would try to win him to the Lord with my Bible rather than do what I could easily do with my hands or a gun.

There is never an excuse for an uncontrolled temper.

Do even good people get angry? Of course. Even Jesus got angry:

John 2:13 *And the Jews' Passover was at hand, and Jesus went up to Jerusalem, 14 And found in the temple those that sold oxen and sheep and doves, and the changers of money sitting: 15 And when he had made a scourge of small cords, he drove them all out of the temple, and the sheep, and the oxen; and poured out the changers' money, and overthrew the tables; 16 And said unto them that sold doves, Take these things hence; make not my Father's house an house*

43

of merchandise. 17 And his disciples remembered that it was written, the zeal of thine house hath eaten me up.

Jesus was furious, rightly so. But look at verse sixteen again to notice how in control He was:

John 2:16 *And said unto them that sold doves, Take these things hence; make not my Father's house an house of merchandise.*

He was so in control, he didn't even scare the doves! He had them carefully carried away.

I know that even women can have a violent temper. And I've known some women that if they got mad could probably squish a guy's head like a grape. But this thing of a violent, uncontrolled, sewage-like temper is mostly the domain of husbands, fathers.

Proverbs 25:28 *He that hath no rule over his own spirit is like a city that is broken down, and without walls.*

Men, women, remove the human waste of uncontrolled temper from your home. Men, you are not being "masculine" by blowing up and scaring people, you are simply demonstrating your own weakness.

Bitterness is human waste.

Hebrews 12:15 *Looking diligently lest any man fail of the grace of God; lest any root of bitterness springing up trouble you, and thereby many be defiled;*

Bitterness is the poisonous result of the refusal to forgive wrongs that have been done to us. When a person gets like that, notice that this verse says *many* will be defiled. Mom, dad, boy, girl, you refuse to forgive, the bitterness that results will defile the rest of the family.

A young couple came to us for counseling. They had had a period of separation, and she had gone and spent some time with an old boyfriend. Now they were back together, and he had a choice to forgive, or hang onto it. He forgave, and they today have one of the sweetest marriages I have ever seen.

Most people, unfortunately, go the other way. Truthfully, some dear people that I know and love are not real big into honestly forgiving and moving on. There are people that have hurt them, and they have given lip-service to forgiving, but have never have actually forgiven the way Christ forgives:

Isaiah 43:25 *I, even I, am he that blotteth out thy transgressions for mine own sake, and* ***will not remember thy sins***.

That is a voluntary choice not to bring things to mind. A home cannot thrive without this, because we all eventually do something that needs to be forgiven! Paul proved that in Romans 3:10

Romans 3:10 *As it is written, There is none righteous, no, not one:*

The only thing that is stopping some of you from having the marriage of your dreams is the fact that you won't forgive!

Let me prove that. People say, "I won't forgive him. He doesn't love me anyway, why should I?" Let me ask this question: why do we love Jesus? Because He forgave us our sins! Which came first? The forgiveness! Nothing breaks a person into loving you quite like unconditional forgiveness.

Self-interest is human waste.

Philippians 2:1 *If there be therefore any consolation in Christ, if any comfort of love, if any fellowship of the Spirit, if any bowels and mercies, 2 Fulfil ye my joy, that ye be likeminded, having the same love, being of one accord, of one mind. 3 Let nothing be done through strife or vainglory; but in lowliness of mind let each esteem other better than themselves. 4 Look not every man on his own things, but every man also on the things of others.*

Truthfully, the more you lose the "me me me" attitude, the more pleasant your life will become:

Acts 20:35 *I have shewed you all things, how that so labouring ye ought to support the weak, and to remember the words of the Lord Jesus, how he said, It is more blessed (makarioi, happy, enjoyable) to give than to receive.*

45

I got to give something recently, and my wife found out about it. Caleb overheard us speaking of it, and he asked about it. I truly enjoyed explaining it, because I want him to learn to be a giver.

In a home, self-interest is a killer:

Like the woman who was willing to clean and cook, but not have sex, because it "wasn't her thing".

Like the man who said, "I work hard, and I don't beat her, what more does she want? (Romeo, Oh, Romeo!)

All of these things, uncontrolled temper, bitterness, self-interest, are nothing more than human waste that needs to be expelled from the home.

PART FOUR:
KEEPING THE WORKERS FROM KILLING EACH OTHER

A beautiful young lady and her old grandpa walked up to the counter at the fabric store. She asked the man working the counter how much a certain fabric would cost. The guy was a dirtbag, and, seeing the pretty girl, he said "aw, that fabric'll cost you one long, wet, kiss per yard." The girl said, "Well, I really do need that fabric. I guess just give me ten yards of it!" The man almost passed out from excitement, but he got himself together and quickly cut the fabric for her. He handed it to her, and said "awright, missy, let's get on with them ten long, wet kisses!" The girl said "No problem! My grandpa pays all my bills anyway." Smart Girl!

When we were building the building, we were really short on help a lot of days. One day, a man came over and brought some of his own workers to help. One of them was smoking. Another man who was there came up to him and snapped "I'd appreciate it if you put out that stinking, nasty cigarette!" The man responded, "If you don't want my help, just say so, and me and my boys will go home!" I quickly intervened, grabbed the snappy guy, pulled him off to the side and said, "Look mister, we are really short handed. That may not mean anything to you, since you'll be gone in a couple more days. But I'll be here working on this thing for the next two years, and I need the help. If that guys murders someone, let me know, and I'll send him home. But as long as he isn't doing anything worse than smoking, find a way to get along with him!"

When you are building a building, or a home, you are going to have times when the workers disagree. In a way, that has been one of the odd blessings of not having many people that have been able to come and help very often on the new church building. I really haven't had to argue about how things ought to look or where they should go or what color they should be! And should anyone who hasn't helped walk into the new building in a few months and go "I don't like the way that part is done, it should have been done the other way" I'll be more than happy to listen to their opinion, and then I'll be more than happy to tell them that they can take their opinion and stuff it! Bless their hearts.

Seriously, though, people do fight and argue. Workers get on each other's nerves, and family members disagree. This has been going on for thousands of years. Look at:

2 Samuel 6:1 *Again, David gathered together all the chosen men of Israel, thirty thousand. 2 And David arose, and went with all the people that were with him from Baale of Judah, to bring up from thence the ark of God, whose name is called by the name of the LORD of hosts that dwelleth between the cherubims. 3 And they set the ark of God upon a new cart, and brought it out of the house of Abinadab that was in Gibeah: and Uzzah and Ahio, the sons of Abinadab, drave the new cart. 4 And they brought it out of the house of Abinadab which was at Gibeah, accompanying the ark of God: and Ahio went before the ark. 5 And David and all the house of Israel played before the LORD on all manner of instruments made of fir wood, even on harps, and on psalteries, and on timbrels, and on cornets, and on cymbals. 6 And when they came to Nachon's threshing floor, Uzzah put forth his hand to the ark of God, and took hold of it; for the oxen shook it. 7*

And the anger of the LORD was kindled against Uzzah; and God smote him there for his error; and there he died by the ark of God. 8 And David was displeased, because the LORD had made a breach upon Uzzah: and he called the name of the place Perezuzzah to this day. 9 And David was afraid of the LORD that day, and said, How shall the ark of the LORD come to me? 10 So David would not remove the ark of the LORD unto him into the city of David: but David carried it aside into the house of Obededom the Gittite. 11 And the ark of the LORD continued in the house of Obededom the Gittite three months: and the LORD blessed Obededom, and all his household. 12 And it was told king David, saying, The LORD hath blessed the house of Obededom, and all that pertaineth unto him, because of the ark of God. So David went and brought up the ark of God from the house of Obededom into the city of David with gladness. 13 And it was so, that when they that bare the ark of the LORD had gone six paces, he sacrificed oxen and fatlings. 14 And David danced before the LORD with all his might; and David was girded with a linen ephod. 15 So David and all the house of Israel brought up the ark of the LORD with shouting, and with the sound of the trumpet. 16 And as the ark of the LORD came into the city of David, Michal Saul's daughter looked through a window, and saw king David leaping and dancing before the LORD; and she despised him in her heart. 17 And they brought in the ark of the LORD, and set it in his place, in the midst of the tabernacle that David had pitched for it: and David offered burnt offerings and peace offerings before the LORD. 18 And as soon as David had made an end of offering burnt offerings and peace offerings, he blessed the people in the name of the LORD of hosts. 19 And he dealt among all the people, even among the whole multitude of Israel, as well to the women as men, to every one a cake of bread, and a good piece of flesh, and a flagon of wine. So all the people departed every one to his house. 20 Then David returned to bless his household. And Michal the daughter of Saul came out to meet David, and said, How glorious was the king of Israel to day, who uncovered himself to day in the eyes of the handmaids of his servants, as one of the vain fellows shamelessly uncovereth himself! 21 And David said unto Michal, It was before the LORD, which chose me before thy father, and before all his house, to appoint me ruler over the people of the LORD, over Israel: therefore will I play before the LORD. 22 And I will yet be more vile than thus, and will be base in mine own sight: and of the maidservants which thou hast spoken of, of them shall I be had in honour. 23 Therefore Michal the daughter of Saul had no child unto the day of her death.

In the days of Eli the priest, he and his two sons had been so wicked before God, that they actually managed to lose the very ark of God to the Philistines for a time. That sacred piece of furniture, made during the wilderness wanderings, was a miniature version of the very mercy seat in heaven where the blood of Jesus Himself would be placed many years later. This earthly ark over the years had had the blood of thousands of sacrifices placed upon it, as God made a covering for the sins of His people. There had never been a more important piece of furniture on earth, yet Israel treated in like a trinket, and lost it to the heathen Philistines. The Philistines did not understand God or the ark, and tens of thousands of them died just by being near it. The ones that didn't die ended up in a condition worse than death (hemorrhoids. Ow.) They finally sent it back to Israel, where it resided in an Israelite's house during the entire reign of Saul, not being brought back into the tabernacle. People were afraid of it. But finally, Saul was dead, David was king, and he began to think of the ark, and the presence of God. He determined to bring it back into the city of David, and set about to do so. But he never bothered to check Scripture first to see how it should be done. As a result, it ended up being carried on a cart instead of on the shoulders of the Levites. When the oxen began to stumble a bit, Uzzah put out his hand to steady the ark, and the moment he touched it, God killed him. That put a stop to David's plans for a while. But a bit later, after he had read the Mosaic law concerning the ark, he determined again to bring the ark back into the city, this time using God's prescribed method to do so. There had never been a greater reclamation project in all of Israel's history. So when David and the people managed to get the ark back into the city, David cut loose celebrating and praising God. He was leaping, and dancing, I mean David was cutting a rug! And on such a joyous occasion, who could blame him? Who but his own wife, that is.

The Bible says in verse sixteen that Michal, the wife of David, looked out of her window. She saw David her husband leaping and dancing before the Lord, and she *despised him in her heart.* That term means she scorned him, she regarded him as worthless, she thought of him in the lowest terms possible. Michal at that point could not possibly have thought any lower of David than she did. But at that point, she was still only despising him in her heart. Not too long later, though, the object of her scorn came home. He had had the greatest day of his life, greater even that the day he slew Goliath, greater than the day he became king. He comes home on cloud nine, and Michal lays into him:

2 Samuel 6:20 *Then David returned to bless his household. And Michal the daughter of Saul came out to meet David, and said, How glorious was the king of Israel to day, who uncovered himself to day in the eyes of the handmaids of his servants, as one of the vain fellows shamelessly uncovereth himself!*

Ooowhoohoo! David has come home to *bless* his household. He has come home to speak wonderful things to them, and Michal just explodes! She mocks him as "glorious," and accuses him of being indecent, vain, and shameless. The marital spat has begun! A home is now hanging in the balance. Look how David responds:

2 Samuel 6:21 *And David said unto Michal, It was before the LORD, which chose me before thy father, and before all his house, to appoint me ruler over the people of the LORD, over Israel: therefore will I play before the LORD. 22 And I will yet be more vile than thus, and will be base in mine own sight: and of the maidservants which thou hast spoken of, of them shall I be had in honour. 23 Therefore Michal the daughter of Saul had no child unto the day of her death.*

Wow! Michal hit David with a 2x4, and David came right back and smacked her with a piece of angle iron. He told her that he was better than her daddy, better than her brothers and cousins, and then told her he was going to be even worse than she accused him of being. From that moment onward, David informed her that she could sleep in her room, he could sleep in his, and she could forget all about that little matter of having kids after that, cause it wasn't gonna happen.

And it didn't. Michal and David were married till death did them part, but they never slept together again. They may have still been married, but their home was destroyed.

What is truly sad about that is that this relationship started out as a true love story. I Samuel 18:20 tells us that while her daddy was king and they were both single, Michal loved David. Verse 27 of that chapter tells us that when Saul asked for the foreskins of 100 Philistines as a dowry for David to marry little miss Michal, David instead went out and killed 200 of them. Verse 28 again says Michal loved him. In chapter 19, she saved his life when her daddy came to kill him. This was a real-life love story. Yet rather than ending with "and they lived happily ever after," it ended with them hating each other's guts. They had a huge fight, and they both lost.

That, friends, is a bad plan all the way around.

Now, there are some things you cannot count on in marriage. You cannot count on the poor husband you married striking it rich. You cannot count on the disorganized wife you married becoming the next Martha Stewart. But one thing that every single marriage can count on is this: there will be times that you disagree. You may or may not verbalize it, you may or may not act on it, but there are not two people anywhere on the planet that think and act the same way about everything all the time. Every couple disagrees sometime. To put it in terms that everyone understands, every couple fights now and then. I didn't say they holler, or scream, or throw things, but they do disagree, and a disagreement is a fight, in the technical sense of the word. But a disagreement does not have to be a harmful thing in a home. If you disagree in a Biblical, Christ-like manner, you will be fine. Here then are some Biblical principles on fighting.

Never fight physically.

1 Corinthians 6:19 *What? know ye not that your body is the temple of the Holy Ghost which is in you, which ye have of God, and ye are not your own?* **20** *For ye are bought with a price: therefore glorify God in your body, and in your spirit, which are God's.*

Physical damage to a child of God is vandalism of God's property. Nobody likes a vandal. When I was eighteen years old, I bought the only new car I have ever owned, a 1988 Honda CRX. It was sky blue, and would run like a scalded dog! One week after I had it, someone took a key, and ran it all the way down the side of it. When I found it the next morning, I had the overwhelming desire to rip someone's face off, in the love of the Lord, of course.

Do you know why nobody likes a vandal? Because vandals are cowards. They pick on helpless people, people who are not there to defend their property. If you men especially beat on a woman, or grab her up, or push her around, please let me, as kindly as I can, tell you what your problem is. Your problem is that you are a panty-waste, sissified, yellow bellied, low life, snot-sucking coward. Your problem is that you cuddle up to a teddy bear each night, and suck your thumb, and still wear potty-training pants. Your problem is you are a weak little loser. Any man that would abuse a woman needs to go see a doctor and find out why he doesn't have all the bodily equipment he's supposed to have.

If you are going to fight to win, rather than to lose, never fight physically. By the way, even women need to listen to me here:

When you pick up kids on a church bus, you will encounter some interesting situations. My bus man called me one night to tell me he had to go up to the jail to see one of the kid's moms. I said, "What in the world did she do?" Turns out she had been having an argument with her husband. He turned around to walk away from her while she was still talking. That was his first mistake. His second mistake (far worse than the first) was not noticing the giant crescent wrench lying on the counter...

Ladies and gentlemen, the first Biblical rule for fighting to win is *never fight physically.* Boys, when you grow up and get married, don't you ever hurt a woman. Brothers and sisters, don't punch and smack each other. The only type of physical pain that ought to be caused in the home is the sting felt on the posterior of a child who gets a much-needed spanking.

Rather than raising your voices, lower them.

Song of Solomon 2:8 *The voice of my beloved! behold, he cometh leaping upon the mountains, skipping upon the hills.*

The dear bride in this passage could not yet see her husband. So what was it in this verse that she was finding attractive? His voice! That brings us to our next rule for fighting, which is to lower voices rather than raise them.

What is one way you can normally tell if people are fighting? *Their raised voices.*

You have no idea how much harm, or how much good, you can do with your tone of voice during a fight. The young lady in the Song of Solomon was taken by *the voice of her beloved.* The tone of voice means something to a mate.

I want to teach you something very interesting:

I will often have a married couple come up and sit in two chairs facing each other. I will inform the crowd that they are "fighting" over the fact that she ran up a $600.00 phone bill calling momma last month. Now, while having them fight, I will have the husband tell the wife, at his shouting best, **"$600.00?!? What in the world were you thinking?"** Then I ask the wife how she knew he was mad. She will refer to his volume.

But then, I will explain the scenario again, and have his say the exact same thing, only have him lower his voice an octave. Does she still know he was mad? How does she know? He wasn't shouting this time, yet something let her know he was mad.

The point is this: it is not a person's volume that lets another person know they are mad. **IF THEY ALWAYS SHOUT, ALL**

DAY EVERYDAY AS A NORMAL WAY OF CONVERSATION, THEN SHOUTING BECOMES NORMAL, AND NOBODY THINKS THEY ARE MAD. It is not a person's volume that communicates anger, it is the change in their volume that does that. So if you can communicate displeasure with a change in your volume, why not change it in such a way that your spouse does not feel threatened or intimidated? If you are going to fight to win, lower your voices rather than raise them. That lets your spouse know that you have not lost control. It lets your spouse know that you are upset, but it also communicates that that you think enough of him or her not to scream.

Use tender names.

Song of Solomon 5:2 *I sleep, but my heart waketh: it is the voice of my beloved that knocketh, saying, Open to me, my sister, my love, my dove, my undefiled: for my head is filled with dew, and my locks with the drops of the night. 3 I have put off my coat; how shall I put it on? I have washed my feet; how shall I defile them? 4 My beloved put in his hand by the hole of the door, and my bowels were moved for him. 5 I rose up to open to my beloved; and my hands dropped with myrrh, and my fingers with sweet smelling myrrh, upon the handles of the lock. 6 I opened to my beloved; but my beloved had withdrawn himself, and was gone: my soul failed when he spake: I sought him, but I could not find him; I called him, but he gave me no answer.*

This is a great passage of Scripture. In verse two, the shepherd spouse knocks on this girl's door late at night, and asks her to come away with him. In verse three, she makes excuses and tells him that she is not going to do what he wants her to do. In other words, by verse three, they are fighting. But in verse four, five, and six, she refers to him as "my beloved!" In the middle of a fight, she uses a tender name for him three straight times.

It is really hard to destroy someone during a fight when you practice this principle.

"Honey, why did you max out the charge card again?"

"Because, sweetie, you only make $4.25 an hour at the burger flipping job you took after you dropped out of school."

"Well, darling honey bun, I wouldn't have had to drop out of school if you hadn't brought your sweet mother to live with us."

"But babycakes, you said you loved my mother."

"I do love your mother, snoockums, but I loved her a lot more when she lived in West Virginia."

What you have just heard is a fight that, apart from those sweet names, could be a real doozy! But God did not give you a mate for you to cut her or him to ribbons with your insulting tongue. No matter how deep the disagreement, you better never use a harsh name or word for the spouse that God has given you. I have heard husbands and wives refer to each other by some of the vilest names imaginable!

Never attack the tender spots.

Philippians 2:3 *Let nothing be done through strife or vainglory; but in lowliness of mind let each esteem other better than themselves.*

This verse teaches another dynamite principle. Even our fights are not to be done through strife, but are to be done in such a way that we are thinking of the welfare of our spouse more than our own welfare. There is no greater way that people violate that principle than by attacking the tender spots.

Here is what I mean: there is one person on earth that you open up to and let into your inner being more than any other, and that is your mate. Husbands, you have the honor of knowing more than anyone else on earth all of the things that your wife is the most sensitive about. Wives, you have the honor of knowing more than anyone else on Earth all of the things that your husband is the most sensitive about:

A boy married a girl with freckles. I mean she had a lot of freckles, and she was very sensitive about them. He told her over and over that he loved them, and that she was beautiful with them. Then, a few years into their marriage, he found himself losing an argument. In the heat of battle, he made the ultimate mistake. He shouted out "I never did like your freckles anyway!" The argument was over that very moment. The fallout lasted for months, as he worked to re-build what he had destroyed.

Husbands and wives, you know more than anyone else the areas that your mate can be easily hurt in, the things that they are sensitive over. You need to make a vow in your heart before God, this very moment, that you will never go after those soft spots during a fight. If you do, you have betrayed them, and they will not trust you for a long, long time, if ever.

Never drop the "5 year bomb".

Ephesians 4:26 *Be ye angry, and sin not: let not the sun go down upon your wrath: 27 Neither give place to the devil.*

This is God's way of putting our fights "under the clock." God forbids us from going to bed with that fight unresolved or un-dropped.

I know beyond a doubt that God's people violate this command, because I continually deal with people who are guilty of dropping the "five year bomb."

What is the five-year bomb? It is that thing that you have been ill about or displeased with for years and years, without your mate even knowing about it. You have been quite, they have no clue, and then in the middle of an argument "I've hated your meatloaf since the day we got married!"

Let me tell you about the fallout from that. You see, with any radioactive weapon, and this is one, the fallout is worse than the initial blast. Here is what this does: when you drop the bomb on your spouse that there is something that you have not liked about them for years, and they did not know about it, what it does is make them wonder what else about them you have always hated. They go from there to wonder if there is even anything about them you have liked, or whether you have only stayed with them because you had to. An overreaction? Yes, but it is the natural fallout from dropping the five year bomb. If you have a problem, deal with it early, but don't ever undermine years of marriage by dropping the five-year bomb.

Treat every disagreement as an individual thing; never bring up the past!

Psalm 103:12 *As far as the east is from the west, so far hath he removed our transgressions from us.*

God is so good to forget what He has forgiven. We, though, are not nearly so good at that.

Married couples tend to store weapons through the years. Every fight, they put that thing in their arsenal, to be used during the next fight. It is no wonder nothing ever gets solved. Old arguments should be just like Elvis: let the nuts of the world think he's alive at the Burger King in Kalamazoo: you let him be dead, because he is. So is every issue you have ever fought over and forgiven. It is dead and gone, leave it buried. A man and wife had gone to a pastor for marriage counseling. The pastor asked them what the problem was. The wife reached down into a bag, and pulled out a big three-ring binder, and flopped it open. She said, "My husband is the problem!" And then she started reading off all of the wrong things he had ever done, no matter how small, and the dates he had done them. The husband kept getting smaller and smaller, sinking down further and further into his chair. Finally, when she was done reading off her husband's faults, she closed the binder smugly. The pastor had been sitting by, listening quietly, but now he spoke. He said, "It is evident from what I just heard read from that book that you are the most self-centered (wife: yeah, yeah!) Arrogant (wife: yeah, yeah!) calloused (wife: yeah, yeah!) UNFORGIVING BITTER OLD WOMAN I HAVE EVER MET! Ma'am, you need to get your heart right with God and learn to forgive and let go of the past!

You go, preacher!

Never air your dirty laundry in public.

Matthew 18:15 *Moreover if thy brother shall trespass against thee, go and tell him his fault between thee and him alone: if he shall hear thee, thou hast gained thy brother.*

This principle about keeping the circle small is a good one. Nothing good ever comes from inviting unqualified others into your fights.

Restaurants are not good forums for airing dirty laundry, no public place is. No body wants to have your smelly socks shoved under their noses! Keep your disagreements within the circle that they need to stay. If you need marriage counseling, go and get it from the pastor. But you have no business going elsewhere:

We had a young couple in the church that was struggling with some issues. Nothing real big, nothing that couldn't be handled. Then one Sunday, she wasn't here. We got to asking, and it turns out she had run home to mama. That's not the worst part. The worst part is, it was another woman in this church (not here anymore) that told her to go run home to mama! I'm counseling them on how to stay together and work through everything and dear Flabber-Jaws is giving the opposite counsel. Dear Flabber-Jaws shouldn't even have been aware of their problems!

Never interrupt.

1 Corinthians 15:33 *Be not deceived: evil communications corrupt good manners.*

Are we not living in the rudest generation ever? Kids being taught to belch out loud. Adults telling kids to call them by their first name. An adult stops by a pew to talk to a young person, and the kid doesn't rise. But this kind of rude behavior carries over into adulthood, especially the practice of interrupting others. Interrupting anyone is not appropriate, but it is especially wicked when we do it to the mate that God has given us. Wait your turn. Actually listen. If you interrupt, it is a sure sign that you aren't even listening to what is being said.

Restate what the other has said in your own words to make sure you understand it.

Proverbs 18:13 *He that answereth a matter before he heareth it, it is folly and shame unto him.*

One of the funniest truths in life is this: you rarely hear what someone actually said. At least as far as they are concerned, you didn't!

The wife says, "Honey, it hurt me when you bought me that vacuum cleaner for our 25th anniversary."

The husband says, "So you are saying that you wanted the ironing board instead?"

No, she wanted the trip to Hawaii instead, Doofus. That is why it is valuable to restate what the other has said in your own words, to make sure you understand it. Not only will this help you to understand, it will also keep you from doing that awful, wicked, sinful thing that most people do during an argument: it will keep you from formulating your own answer while your mate is still speaking. When you do that, you are not listening. You only have one teeny brain, and it cannot truly listen at the exact same time it is readying its own speech.

So many problems in the home come as a result of not hearing what people meant. It is one thing to hear what they said, another to hear what they meant. You see, what they are saying may mean something different coming out of their brain than it does entering into your brain. Men, women, have you ever felt like you were both speaking English but talking a completely different language?

There is an old quote that sums it up pretty well: I know you believe you understand what you think I said, but I'm not sure you realize that what you heard is not what I meant.

Does that often sound like your home? So restate things in your own words to make sure!

About that "last word": If who gets the last word is an issue, solve it by agreeing now that the last word will always be an unreserved positive.

1 Corinthians 16:23 *The grace of our Lord Jesus Christ be with you. 24 My love be with you all in Christ Jesus. Amen.*

May I point out something amazing? Paul wrote a letter to the Church at Corinth. He chewed them out for a bazillion different things, including fornication, adultery, abuse of the Lord's supper, misuse of the spiritual gifts, failing to exercise church discipline, you name it, he had to blast them for it. But at the end of the letter, at the end of the "fight," if you will, he said, "The grace of our Lord Jesus Christ be with you. My love be with you all in Christ Jesus." There was not a hint of negativity in that!

You know how we usually end an argument? Honey, I love you, but . . .

Baby, I forgive you, but...

Leave off the but. Every fight needs to end with an unreserved positive.

How many times have you heard people complain "you always have to have the last word!" How many of you are married to someone who always has to have the last word? Let them have it. This will fix this forever. If you both agree now that the last word will always- always- always be an unreserved positive, than who gets the last word will not matter anymore.

Being reconciled is far more important than being right.

Matthew 5:24 *Leave there thy gift before the altar, and go thy way; first be reconciled to thy brother, and then come and offer thy gift.*

This one principle, the most important one, I have saved for last. If you forget everything else, please remember this: being reconciled is far more important than being right. In any fight, both sides go into it thinking that they are right, and the other is wrong, otherwise, they would not be fighting! But when all is said and done,

61

you can curl up and go to sleep with your spouse, or you can curl up and go to sleep with your pride. Buddy, choose whatever you want, but pride never gave anybody a hickey!

Who was wrong? Michal and David battled it out, and a home was destroyed. Was Michal wrong? Yes. Was David wrong? Yes. If you are going to build a strong home, the workers need to make sure that they "fight nice."

PART FIVE:
ELIMINATING ENEMIES FROM BELOW

A lady named Valerie Runyon tells this story: She said, "Soon after our last child left home for college, my husband was resting next to me on the couch with his head in my lap. I carefully removed his glasses. "You know, honey," I said sweetly, "without your glasses you look like the same handsome young man I married." "Honey," he replied with a grin, "without my glasses, you still look pretty good too!"

What do you want to bet they had to have some marriage counseling?

There is so much that went into our building underneath the slab that would just blow your mind. We built a metal building, with metal studs, covered in drywall, with a concrete foundation. But before we could pour the slab, we had to treat for termites! Now I don't know what your experience is, but in my experience, most termites don't like to chew on metal or concrete. I can just see some little termite sitting in a dentist's chair, having dentures and braces installed, going, "Well doc, I was hungry, and those metal studs looked pretty good..."

Regardless, we had to spend $750.00 treating the ground for termites before we could pour the slab. The inspector explained that if we didn't, those termites could come up through any little gap, and chew on pews, or platform, or whatever they could get their little bicuspids on.

Not only did we have to treat for termites before we could pour the slab, we also had to cover the entire grade with heavy plastic. The reason we did that was to protect against ground moisture. You see, if you just pour a slab right onto the gravel on the ground, moisture will seep up through the concrete, and literally soak the floor inside the building! That can cause rotting, and mold, and a host of other nasty issues. So to protect against that, we put nearly $1000.00 of plastic on the ground, and covered it in concrete.

We will never again see the poison under the slab. We will never again see the plastic under the slab. But those things aren't there for us to see, they are there to give us some protection from the enemies that the earth itself harbors or produces.

Now let's take that thought and transition into the next thought. The world itself produces things that are damaging to our homes. It does so especially in regards to our children. It's up to us to do some preventative maintenance to protect our children from what the world produces! So let's look at a few harmful things the world produces, and how to protect our kids from them.

A pressure to grow up too quickly.

1 Corinthians 13:11 *When I was a child, I spake as a child, I understood as a child, I thought as a child: but when I became a man, I put away childish things.*

Kids are supposed to be kids. That is basically what Paul just said.

But the pressure from the world is to make them enter the adult world and do adult things while they are still kids. Kids aren't equipped to handle adult things.

Have you noticed how kids today don't usually seem like kids anymore? It used to be an eight or nine year old was up early to watch Bugs Bunny and Roadrunner on Saturday, and then it was out into the yard to play. When they got a little crush, they would hand a buddy a cheesy little note to give to sweet thing that said "I like you, do you like me, check yes or no." Then if they got a no, they erased out the mark in the "no" box, and recycled the note to someone else. They giggled and blushed, and didn't know any bad words. The facts of life were as follows: girls have cooties, boys are icky.

My how things have changed… Our kids are under pressure to look like little adults (Beauty pageants, modeling...)

I have no problem with "beautiful baby" contests. I have no problems with "cute little kid" contests. But I have a very real problem with "beauty pageants." I have problems with taking a little girl, dressing her like a woman, covering her in makeup, and making a six year old look like a twenty-six year old. I have a real problem with turning kids into bait for pedophiles. I have a real problem with taking a kid who should be about half-tomboy and turning her into a tart.

It's the same for little boys. Little boys have no business being dressed up like men and dragged around looking for modeling contracts.

We ought to be teaching our children to seek God in all the simplicity of youth, but instead people are teaching them to focus on their own made-up beauty.

Last year, the news in Charlotte reported on a local fourteen year old girl who was doing swimsuit modeling. They said she was going to be the next big sensation. Fourteen years old! When her father was interviewed, he said "well, I'm a little bit uncomfortable with how I know full grown men are looking at my little girl, but this is her chance to make it big, and I'm not going to discourage her." God have mercy! God have mercy when a dad doesn't have any more sense than to encourage his little girl to parade around in things no adult woman should even be wearing in public!

Moms and dads, you need to understand that the world and the devil are going to put your kids under enormous pressure to look like little adults. You need to be the termite poison under the slab that keeps them from getting eaten alive.

Our kids are under pressure to develop adult type relationships. Kids have always wanted to do the "go steady get married early thing." The difference is, adults, and even a lot of parents, are now pushing them to do it!

I have almost lost count of the number of times I have heard adults talking about their 10, 11, 12 year olds, saying, "Well my daughter has a little boyfriend, my son has a little girlfriend..."

Oh, I don't think so! That kind of thing isn't "cute" it's insane!

That's what God gave kids parents for, to throw a t-mortal hissy fit (which is far more severe than just an ordinary hissy-fit) and say "at your age you can have books, you can have bats and balls and gloves, you can have an occasional video game that I get to choose, but you do not now, nor will you for a very long time, have a boyfriend or a girlfriend!"

Kids can't handle those types of relationships yet. Their hormones are stronger than their will power. They can't handle the emotional entanglements either. God designed youth for a specific reason:

Ecclesiastes 12:1 *Remember now thy Creator in the days of thy youth...*

There is no better time than youth for developing a really close relationship with God, and there is no worse time than youth for developing a really close relationship with a member of the opposite sex! That is an enemy from below that you need to guard against. Parents, you need to lay down the law often and early on this. Start when they are four and five, and don't let up on this.

There are so many other ways that our kids are under pressure to grow up too quickly. And one of the things that makes it possible is that parents have stopped trying to be real parents, and have listened to psychologists and are now trying to be "buddies" with their kids. I am a friend, I hope the very best friend, to my children. But I am their father first and foremost. Dana is their mother first and foremost. We make it clear every day that they are the kids and we are the adults. What we think means more than what they think, because we know more than they know, and we pay all the bills. They are not allowed to back talk. When they disobey, they are punished. I am not trying to place them on my level, nor will I lower myself to theirs. The only way kids can truly be kids is if their parents are truly adults! We decide what clothes make it from the store to their closet. They don't even get a vote in the matter. We decide what their bedtime is, and if they whine about it, they march in place till they get tired enough to like the idea of going to bed. We decide where they will go and what they will do. And because we are real parents, they can afford to be real kids!

Do we play with them? All the time. Yesterday, we were out in the yard shooting off their pump-up air rocket. But when it came time to go in, we ordered them into the house. They don't have to deal with the pressure of scheduling, or budgeting their allowance, or figuring out what style of clothes they should be wearing or what hairstyles they should have. They can afford to play and be kids, because we decide all those things for them. We have decreed that they will not have boyfriends or girlfriends till we are ready for that for them. We have decreed that they will dress and act like kids. We will not let them grow up too quickly, and they are not big enough to do anything about it. They may not thank us now. They may not even like us from time to time. Makes no difference. I'm a dad, and some times my job requires me to make them unhappy. I love my job, because I know they'll be better off if I do it right.

Here is another harmful thing the world produces:

An education system that is inadequate at best, dangerous at worse.

Proverbs 4:23 *Keep (guard, blockade, keep soldiers stationed about) thy heart with all diligence; for out of it are the issues of life.*

Young kids are too easily influenced to keep their hearts; you need to do it for them.

May I point out a mathematical problem that you parents ought to consider? How many hours a week do your kids spend in church where a pastor teaches them? Three or four. Except for home-schoolers, how many hours a week do you actually spend teaching your kids things? Maybe three or four at most. But how many hours a week are they in school, being taught by someone other than a pastor, and other than you? Around forty. And that doesn't include homework, or ISS for our "more difficult" children.

In other words, the school system has ten times as much time to influence them as you and I do.

Parents, do you think it is wise to just send them off to school for twelve years and hope for the best? I don't think so. If anyone besides me is going to have that much influence over my kids, I want to know what is being taught, and if it isn't right, I want it changed, or I am taking my kid elsewhere.

A moment ago I described the American educational system as inadequate at best, dangerous at worse. That doesn't mean every school or every teacher is terrible. It doesn't mean that every student comes out an incompetent moron. But there are some things you just cannot deny:

Lots of kids are graduating hardly able to read the diplomas they are handed.

Textbooks are filled with historical and grammatical errors.
Here are a few historical errors:

"Columbus first reached North America in 1492." Columbus never reached North America. He explored Caribbean islands and the northern coast of South America.

"James Monroe was the last president to have fought in the Revolutionary War." Andrew Jackson, not James Monroe, was the last president to have fought in the American Revolution.

"The Fourteenth Amendment extended the right to vote to all 21-year-old males, including former slaves." It was the Fifteenth Amendment that gave blacks the right to vote.

"Before the Civil War, greenbacks were redeemable for either gold or silver coins." There were no greenbacks before the Civil War. They originated during the war with the 1862 Legal Tender Act.

Here are a few from science textbooks:

A map showing the equator running through Texas and Florida, although the equator is about 1,500 miles south of the southern United States.

A discussion of sound that claims humans cannot hear below 400 hertz, but 47 notes on the piano are below 400 hertz.

A description of the Statue of Liberty explaining her "bronze outer structure." The statue is copper.

A compass with east and west reversed.

Simplified chemistry formulas and physics laws that are completely wrong.

Pictures of prisms bending light the wrong way.

These are the textbooks kids are *still* learning from!

Schools are often more interested in social engineering, like racial quotas, than they are in actual education. A kid will ride a bus for two hours to go to a school across the county instead of the one right by the house just to make sure enough people of different races go to schools together, regardless of the fact that those hours on the bus could be spent studying instead.

Sex education, which should happen in the home under godly Christian parents, is taught by strangers in school at early ages with the world's view instead of God's view

The *theory* of evolution is taught as a scientific fact, and anyone who even dares question it on scientific or Biblical grounds will lose his/her job.

A teacher can take your kid for an abortion and never tell you, but right here in Cleveland County, North Carolina, I have a copy of a note that a teacher sent to a parent forbidding a child to carry *lip balm* in her purse, since it is regarded as a medication!

The Bible isn't allowed, prayer isn't allowed, and in many cases even the pledge of allegiance isn't allowed anymore.

Our kids are often graduating as full-fledged liberal, godless, uneducated heathens, with no morality left within them. Years ago a Marxist said, "You can have the pulpits. Give me the schools, and in one generation I will control the world."

Any time this subject comes up, lots of parents get a sinking feeling in the pit of their stomach, because they feel like they are trapped, they feel like they can't afford any other option than the status quo. Parents, may I make some suggestions?

First of all, be willing to examine other options. Don't just automatically assume that you can't do anything else:

Proverbs 18:13 *He that answereth a matter before he heareth it, it is folly and shame unto him.*

As I have talked to parents through the years, let me tell you what I have never yet heard. I have never yet heard a parent say: *"you know, we have the money and the option to send our kids anywhere, public school, Christian school, private school, or to stay home and home school, and we have decided that out of all those options, public school is the very best option for our kids."*

There may be some parents that feel that way, but I have surely never met one who said so. What I have met often are parents that would like another option, but don't feel like they have another option. But my encouragement is for you to check very carefully. Maybe you do have an option. Maybe within a year or two or careful budgeting, you could have another option.

It might just be an option for you to send your kid to Christian school. You'll never know until you check it out! Maybe if you pray, really pray about it, and make adjustments to the budget, maybe you could swing it after all.

It might just be an option for you to home school. Lots of our parents do it. My wife has our five-year-old daughter reading at a sixth grade level! You may make a pretty good teacher.

Maybe at this time you just find that you cannot do anything other than public school. If that is the case, you should take it upon yourself to know everything your child is being taught, and correct any of the errors. You should speak up at school board meetings against bad textbooks and bad teachers. If they are going to hold your kids in their hands, you need to hold their feet to the fire!

But what happens is, the school system gets so big and so powerful, strong parents suddenly get scared to confront it. If I taught your kids some of the things they get taught in schools, you would have words with me. If I decided that your kids should miss church because I say so, you would have words with me. But how many "Christian" parents have had words with the school system here in Cleveland county, which last year scheduled a graduation on Wednesday night, and often requires kids to miss a Sunday night or Wednesday night for other reasons?

You need to remember that they are county employees, you pay their salary with your taxes, and they work for you.

Parents, if anyone is going to have ten times as much time to influence your kids as you do, you better be the plastic under the slab that keeps your kids safe.

Here is another harmful thing the world produces:

A youth culture that produces a rebellion against the things of God.

Romans 12:1 *I beseech you therefore, brethren, by the mercies of God, that ye present your bodies a living sacrifice, holy, acceptable unto God, which is your reasonable service.* **2** *And be not conformed to this world: but be ye transformed by the renewing of your mind, that ye may prove what is that good, and acceptable, and perfect, will of God.*

It is not God's will for you or me or any of our kids to fit into a wicked culture. This culture at this time does not produce respect for the things of God, it produces rebellion against the things of God:

Most of what comes on TV will produce a rebellion against the things of God. If you let your kids watch shows where unmarried people sleep together, please don't cry later when your own kid strips down and gives away her own purity.

If you let your kids watch shows where kids are disrespectful, don't be surprised when they sass and back talk you.

They soak in what they see and hear like sponges, and it will come out in their lives!

Most of the music the youth of today loves will produce a rebellion against the things of God.

Parents, even your lily-white, southern hick kids are getting into a form of music that you would be shocked by. As bad as rock was and still is, as bad as much country was and still is, a lot of kids sitting on Baptist church pews this morning are getting into rap and hip-hop music. I defy you to find any good that comes out of that. I defy you to find one kid that ever got on fire for God through it. I defy you to find one kid who ever became more respectful to their parents by listening to it. I defy you to find one teenager who developed a healthy respect for law enforcement from it.

If you watch your kids, they will often make some of the same hand gestures as those hip-hop punks do. I have seen some pretty familiar kids online making gang related hand signals. All of this comes from the filthy, rap and hip hop movement.

Kids, if you listen to that garbage, you are not right with God, you may not even be saved!

Parents, if you let them listen to it, you have gone nuts!

Most of what kids do or see online, be it on Myspace, Facebook, or others, will produce a rebellion against the things of God. Parents, if any of you doubt this, come to us. We will take you on a little tour of the online world of young people. In ten minutes, we can show you enough to make you sick at your stomach.

72

Most of the popular sports stars of the day will produce a rebellion against the things of God. I love sports, but I cannot think of a single sports star that I want my kid emulating!

NASCAR stars with beer logos on their car are hardly good role models. NBA heros that produce illegitimate children in each town they visit are not people I want my kids to be like. Wrestling? Don't even go there. If you watch or let your kids watch that pornographic, blasphemous, cursing filled bunch of filth, you shouldn't even wait till the end of a message to hit the altar.

We had a kid come to our church a few years ago wearing an "Austin 3:16: shirt." I went ballistic.

Most of the clothing foisted on our kids will produce a rebellion against the things of God. The Bible teaches modesty, yet clothes producers make clothes with writing across the tail. The Bible teaches modesty, yet clothes producers every year make things higher on the bottom, lower at the top, tighter all over, and about 80 percent see through. This isn't going to help you with your kids. You need to shop carefully, or maybe learn how to sew! Years ago, it wouldn't have mattered what Belks or the GAP produced, because mamas and grandmas would just pull out the old Singer sewing machine and go to town!

Many of the video games of today will produce a rebellion against the things of God. We have come a long way from Pac Man, Defender, Space Invaders, and Donkey Kong. Did you know that video games now have ratings, like movies? They have become so violent, so bloody, so pornographic, that they are rated.

GA for general audience. Appropriate for all audiences. No blood or graphic violence. No profanity, no mature sexual themes and no usage of drugs or alcohol. Examples of games with this rating were Disney's Aladdin, Ecco the Dolphin, Earthworm Jim, Sonic the Hedgehog 3 and most sports and puzzle games

MA for mature audiences. The game was suitable for audiences thirteen years of age or older. Game could have some blood in it and more graphic violence than a "GA" game. Examples of games with this rating were Bram Stoker's Dracula, Flashback: The Quest for Identity, Super Street Fighter II, Lunar: The Silver Star, Wing Commander.

MA-17 for Mature Audiences: Not appropriate for minors. The game was "suitable" for audiences seventeen years of age or older. Games could have lots of blood, graphic violence, mature sexual themes, profanity, drug or alcohol usage. Examples of games with this rating were: Leisure Suit Larry 6: Shape Up or Slip Out!, Lethal Enforcers, Mortal Kombat II, Rise of the Dragon and the Sega CD version of Mortal Kombat among others.

Some of your kids are playing games like this! They are not appropriate for any age at all!

Be not conformed to this world... be transformed... let your mind be renewed.

This is all still basic foundational. If you don't handle these things, it will produce disaster for years to come.

PART SIX:
ANCHOR BOLTS

S omeone has just opened a new store in Charlotte NC. What could go wrong with that? It is a very unique store; it is called "The Husband Store." It is where single women go to buy husbands.

A woman who wanted a husband went to that store. When she walked in on the basement level, she noticed that there was a sign in the lobby with some rules that every customer had to follow. Here were the rules: One, you can only pick one husband. Two, there are five floors. Once you have been to a floor, you cannot come back to it. Three, once you have picked a husband, or been to the last floor, you have to leave, and you cannot come back.

This woman read the rules, understood them, and then hopped into the elevator and went on up to the first floor. When she got to the first floor, she read the sign that said, "Welcome to the first floor. All of the husbands on this floor are born-again Christians. She said, "Wow, I've always wanted a Christian husband! But I wonder what's on the second floor?

On she went to the second floor. When she got there, the sign said, "Welcome to the second floor. All of the men on this floor are born-again Christians, and all of them are hard-working with good, steady jobs." "Wow," the woman said, "What could be better than a man that is saved, and hard working with a good, steady job?" I ought to get a husband from this floor. Still, I wonder what's on the next floor?"

On she went to the third floor. When she got there, that sign read "Welcome to the third floor. All of the men on this floor are born-again Christians, all of them are hard-working with good, steady jobs, and all of them love children and help with the housework." "Whoa!" Said the woman, what in the world could be better than a man who is a born-again Christian, is hard-working with a good steady job, loves children and helps with the housework? But if this floor has such great men for husbands, what must the next floor have?"

So on she went to the fourth floor. There, the sign read "Welcome to the fourth floor. All of the men on this floor are born-again Christians, all of them are hard-working with good steady jobs, all of them love children and help with the housework, and all of them have rippling muscles, washboard abs, and a full head of hair." "Oh my goodness," said the woman. "This is too much. There is no way any man could be better than a born-again Christian who is hard-working with a good steady job, loves children and helps with the housework, and has rippling muscles, washboard abs, and a full head of hair! I know I should march right in and pick out a husband this instant. But if the men on this floor are this awesome, what must the men on the next floor be like?"

So off she went to the fifth and final floor. When she got there, the sign read "Welcome to the fifth floor of The Husband Store. You are the 5,387, 231st customer to visit this floor. There are no men on this floor. This floor exists just to prove that you can never satisfy a woman."

It was a blessed day to me when we finally got done with all of the site preparation, laying out of the footers, septic system, termite poison and plastic, and actually poured the foundation for the building. That is the day I finally felt like we were getting somewhere, seeing that big beautiful slab lying on the ground. But it is interesting that there was some pretty significant metal sticking up out of the slab. You see, a thick, smooth slab is of no use whatsoever unless you have some way to attach the building to the slab. So before we poured that slab, we did some things. We laid out heavy mesh metal wire all over the plastic, and tied it all together with metal ties. Then we welded rebar together to make grade beams, put them into the footer trenches, and used the metal ties to attach the rebar beams to the wire mesh. Then we welded huge anchor bolts to the rebar, which was attached to the wire mesh. Those anchor bolts stuck several inches up above the slab. When we attached our main beams to those anchor bolts, we literally attached them to every single piece of metal under and inside the slab itself! That building is very unlikely to ever blow away, no matter how hard the winds may blow.

There have always been, and will always be, severe winds blowing against the homes that God has given us. That being the case, there needs to be some things that anchor us down, and keep us from being blown away.

It is ironic that today as I preach, it is father's day, because this chapter will be one of the chapters in this book where we deal with fathers. You see, ideally, the father in a home should fulfill the same role as the anchor bolts in that foundation. You fathers need to hear this. You unmarried boys need to hear this, because one day this will be the role you are called on to fill. You wives need to hear this, so you will be able to support your husband while he fulfills this difficult role. You girls need to hear it so you will know what to look for in a potential husband one day. You single moms need to hear it too, because you find yourself in the unenviable position of having to take much of this task on yourself.

A father, like an anchor bolt, needs to be tied in deeply to a strong foundation

Matthew 7:24 *Therefore whosoever heareth these sayings of mine, and doeth them, I will liken him unto a wise man, which built his house upon a rock: 25 And the rain descended, and the floods came, and the winds blew, and beat upon that house; and it fell not: for it was founded upon a rock. 26 And every one that heareth these sayings of mine, and doeth them not, shall be likened unto a foolish man, which built his house upon the sand: 27 And the rain descended, and the floods came, and the winds blew, and beat upon that house; and it fell: and great was the fall of it.*

In the account Christ cited, why did one house not fall, while the other one did? Both houses went through heavy rains; there was no difference in that. Both houses were beset by a flood; there was no difference in that. Both houses were assailed by high winds; there was no difference in that.

The circumstances were the same; the only difference was the foundation. Dads, if your home is going to survive and thrive, you need to be tied in deeply to a strong foundation. It is your job more than anyone else in the home to be the anchor bolt, and to be dug in so deeply to a strong foundation that your home becomes too strong to fall.

I encourage wives to be stable and steady and dug in deeply to a personal walk with Christ. I encourage kids to be stable and steady and dug in deeply to a personal walk with Christ. I EXPECT fathers, I EXPECT FATHERS to be stable and steady and dug in deeply to a personal walk with Christ. Men, it is your job... God will hold you personally responsible for how your family thrives or suffers due to your walk with Christ or lack of a walk with Christ.

It is a shame and a tragedy when men who claim to be Christians have such a shallow walk with Christ, if any at all. Men, your wives and kids should not have to lead in spiritual things. They ought to be able to follow your example in spiritual things. It always flabbergasts me when some hair-covered oaf says: "aight woman, you and the kids git yoursevs up and git ta the church hayuws. I aint gonna raise no heathens. I'll be sittin right here drinkin a brew and watchin the race when ya git back..."

You sorry sack of horse snot. You're a disgrace to the name of fatherhood. It is your job to be reading your Bible every day, praying every day, despising and avoiding sin every day. It is your job to make sure both you and the family are up and out of the house heading for church every time the doors are open. It is your job to pray with and over your kids and your wife. It is your job to be the anchor bolt of the home, dug deeply into a personal walk with Christ. If you aren't anchored deeply into a walk with Christ, your family is either going to have to try and do your job for you, or they are going to fall when adversity comes.

Jonathan Edwards had a deep, personal walk with Christ. He knew Him, he loved Him, and he walked with Him every day. You know Jonathan Edwards the man, the preacher, the one who preached <u>Sinners in the Hands of an Angry God</u>. But he was also Jonathan Edwards the husband, Jonathan Edwards the father, Jonathan Edwards the grandfather. A few years ago, a reporter did a study of his descendants, to see what his personal walk with Christ had produced. Here is what they found:

> 13 college presidents. 100 lawyers. 66 doctors. 65 university professors. 2 university deans. 80 holders of public office, including 3 senators and three state governors. 135 published authors. Countless missionaries and preachers. Every known descendant was considered a great reader and highly intelligent. The reporter concluded by saying "The family has cost the country nothing in pauperism, in crime, in hospital or asylum service: on the contrary, it represents the highest usefulness."[1]

Men, if you want to have a home where you can look back from heaven and be proud of several generations, there is no substitute for you being and anchor bolt dug deeply into a personal relationship with Christ!

A father, like an anchor bolt, needs to be pretty much unbendable

Joshua 24:15 *And if it seem evil unto you to serve the LORD choose you this day whom ye will serve; whether the gods which your fathers served that were on the other side of the flood, or the gods of the Amorites, in whose land ye dwell: but as for me and my house, we will serve the LORD.*

Do you realize in one way how hilarious this verse is, especially in light of our "modern age?" Joshua spoke for himself... and his kids... and his wife!

Can you imagine a man with a "modern, liberated family" doing this?

"Mr. President, you've been a liberal your whole life, but recently you got saved. How has your family reacted to this?"

"Well, neither Hillary nor Chelsea are real pleased by it, but I just figure they'll have to get over it. As for me and my house, we will serve the Lord. I've told Hillary to quit supporting abortion and homosexuality, to give up her Senate seat, and to come home and clean the house. I threw out all of Chelsea's tight, immodest clothes, and bought her a bunch of nice, pretty, modest dresses and skirts. Next week, I'm taking her out of Harvard, and sending her to Hyles-Anderson Christian college. I also got rid of a bunch of Hillary's books. "The Feminine Mystique" by Gloria Steinem, Al Gore's "Earth In The Balance", (Can you believe anybody buys than junk?) and I put a bunch of King James Bibles all over the house.

Yeah, but that's not the best of it. Just wait till next month when they find out I'm sending them down to Sammy Allen's camp meeting for vacation..."

Whew! Wouldn't you love to see that interview?

Joshua spoke for all of his house, and proclaimed that from the youngest to the oldest, all of them would serve the Lord.

Now stop and think of this. How likely do you think it is that the wife and kids of Joshua never bucked him a single time? Not likely at all. You know there were times when Joshua had to put them in line, and you know they did not always care for it. Do you know what it takes to get the job done when you have chosen that both you and your family will serve the Lord? It takes a father who is pretty much unbendable on the things that matter:

Men, be men! Decide some things early on, and then don't ever bend.

In our home (and yes, my wife has helped in the decision making process, but ultimately, the decisions are mine) I've already decided what kinds of kids my kids will be allowed to court when they get older. I've already decided that as long as they live in my house, they will be in church every time the doors are open. I've already decided that they will not be allowed to back talk or be disrespectful. I've already decided on what kind of clothes they will be allowed to wear. I've already decided that and a whole bunch of other things for them, and they won't even get a vote in the matter.

Let me tell you how to do this:

First of all, start early. That which kids grow up with is what they consider normal. My kids already know that daddy is in charge, and as long as I never give an inch, that will be perfectly normal to them. Maybe some of you started a little late, maybe you didn't know better while your kids were little. You have some catching up to do. You can do it, but it won't be easy. You, who have little kids, start early. And moms, if you want your home to be right, back you husbands up all the way in the role of authority God has given him!

Secondly, develop thick skin. My kids love me; they tell me so often. They hug me and kiss me. But you know what? There are also a lot of times we sit down to eat, and every one of them decides they want to sit by mommy. In fact, it is usually that way! Daddy is usually the one enforcing the rules, and they tend to like mommy a lot more than me! That's fine. My job isn't to be liked. My job is to be an unbendable anchor bolt holding things in place.

Thirdly, be just as quick to play and praise, as you are to punish.

A young man was to be sentenced to the penitentiary. The judge had known him from childhood, for he was well acquainted with his father – a famous legal scholar, and the author of a great book on the law. "Do you remember your father?" asked the magistrate. "I remember him well, your honor," came the reply. Then, trying to probe the offender's conscience, the judge said, "As you are about to be sentenced and as you think of your wonderful dad, what do you remember most clearly about him?" There was a pause. Then the judge received an answer he had not expected. "I remember when I went to him for advice. He looked up at me from the book he was writing and said, 'Run along, boy; I'm busy!' When I went to him for companionship, he turned me away, saying "Run along, son; this book must be finished!' Your honor, you remember him as a great lawyer. I remember him as a lost friend." The magistrate muttered to himself, "Alas! Finished the book, but lost the boy!"

Charles Francis Adams, the 19th century political figure and diplomat, kept a diary. One day he entered: "Went fishing with my son today – a day wasted." His son, Brook Adams, also kept a diary, which is still in existence. On that same day, Brook Adams made this entry: "Went fishing with my father – the most wonderful day of my life!"

Dads, you are the anchor bolt in your home. Read your Bible, make the decisions for your kids that God expects you to make, and then be unbendable!

A father, like an anchor bolt, needs to hold things steady through every storm

Acts 20:22 *And now, behold, I go bound in the spirit unto Jerusalem, not knowing the things that shall befall me there: 23 Save that the Holy Ghost witnesseth in every city, saying that bonds and afflictions abide me. 24 **But none of these things move me**, neither count I my life dear unto myself, so that I might finish my course with* *joy, and the ministry, which I have received of the Lord Jesus, to testify the gospel of the grace of God.*

1 Corinthians 15:58 *Therefore, my beloved brethren, be ye stedfast,* **unmoveable**, *always abounding in the work of the Lord, forasmuch as ye know that your labour is not in vain in the Lord.*

Paul went through a lot of storms, and stayed steady through them all. He was unmoveable.

We had a massive wind storm a couple of months ago. Trees down everywhere, shingles blowing off of roofs, lots of damage. Our new building is up on a hill, with no trees to protect it. If it had just been sitting on that slab, it would be in Rutherford County. The only reason it is still in place is the anchor bolts!

Dad, the fact that you have kids means that you are going to have storms. It is comparatively easy to be strong and steady during the easy times, but your family needs you to be strong and steady during the storms.

When you and momma are not quite getting along, your family still needs you to be a strong and steady anchor bolt, doing what is right and holding things together.

When the family finances are not doing so well, your family needs you to be a strong and steady anchor bolt, doing what is right and holding things together.

When your precious babies become *teenagers*, your family needs you to be a strong and steady anchor bolt, doing what is right and holding things together.

When a loved on dies, your family needs you to be a strong and steady anchor bolt, doing what is right and holding things together.

Whatever the storm, your family needs you to be a strong and steady anchor bolt, doing what is right and holding things together.

I have often longed to have a human father to turn to in the storms, and never have. But God has impressed upon my heart that most males get two chances to experience what a father should be like. If you did not *have* a good father, you can at least *be* a good father.

A father, like an anchor bolt, needs to be in it for the long haul.

Psalm 37:25 *I have been young, and now am old; yet have I not seen the righteous forsaken, nor his seed begging bread.*

Psalm 37 was written by David. You can't deny that David messed up pretty badly on occasion. But you also can't deny that he started serving God as a young child, and was still as steady as a rock when he died as an old man.

Lots, and I mean LOTS of dads, make a little profession, last for a while serving God and doing right, and then go right back to their old sin. They're about as long lasting as a campaign promise. We are dealing right now with the fallout from a man just like this. I can give you a tape of him preaching a really good message a few years ago. Probably the best thing we could do is play it for him next weekend while he's laid out drunk. His kids were on fire for God, not nearly so much so now. Had he stayed steady, that family would be incredible right now. None of this is a secret, it is known by all.

Men, five years from now, ten years from now, twenty years from now, unless we have demolished the building and ripped them up with an excavator, those anchor bolts will still be there, doing there job. Thirty or forty years from now, they will still be there doing their job.

How about you? Next year at this time, will you still be holding steady? How about five years from now...Ten? Twenty? Men, you should go all the way to your grave being the spiritual anchor bolt for your home. If you "take time off," lives will be ruined.

> *His shoulders are a little bent,*
> *His youthful force a trifle spent,*
> *But he's the finest man I know,*
> *With heart of gold and hair of snow.*
> *He's seldom cross and never mean;*

He's always been so good and clean;
I only hope I'll always be
As kind to him as he's to me.
Sometimes he's tired and seems forlorn,
His happy face is lined and worn;
Yet he can smile when things are bad:
That's why I like my gray-haired dad.
He doesn't ask the world for much--
Just comfort, friendliness, and such;
But from the things I've heard him say,
I know it's up to me to pay
For all the deeds he's done for me
Since I sat rocking on his knee;
Oh, not in dollars, dimes, or cents--
That's not a father's recompense;
Nor does he worship wealth and fame--
He'd have me honor Jesus' name.
~ Author Unknown ~

Hang in there, men, you are the anchor bolts of your home!

PART SEVEN:
BRINGING THE MAIN BEAMS TOGETHER

T he main beams of our building amaze me. I did not realize ahead of time that those huge creations come in separate pieces, and have to be put together. There are two matching pieces that have to be brought together just right. When the building is done, they will still be joined together. You won't see them though. They will be out of sight, out of mind, but they will be joined together from now on, and that strong union, unseen by the world, will serve as a source of strength for the entire structure.

That to me is such a great picture of the relationship between man and wife, who together make up the main beams of the home.
Hebrews 13:4 *Marriage is honourable in all, and the bed undefiled: but whoremongers and adulterers God will judge.*

Perhaps you have not figured this out yet, but most of us fundamental preachers love hammering on the negative:

If you dirty rotten homosexuals don't get saved, you're going to hell!

If you don't tithe, you're a filthy robber of God, and you are going to go bankrupt, blind, and bald!

87

You scoundrels that are out there gossiping, you need to lay that old wicked tongue of yours on this altar, even if it has to hang off both sides of it!

Oh yes, friends, we love preaching on the negative. It feels good to swing the sword, we like taking down the enemy, and so much of the Bible does deal with negatives. But it also deals with a great many positive subjects, sometimes in the very same verse as a negative one. For instance, in our text verse, Hebrews 13:4, there is an undeniably negative portion that preachers rightfully deal with on a regular basis: *whoremongers and adulterers God will judge.* Oh how true that is, and how necessary it is for the man of God to fearlessly proclaim it.

But there is also a very positive portion to this verse: *Marriage is honorable in all, and the bed undefiled.* When we deal with the negative portion of this verse, we are dealing with the *defiled* bed. We are dealing with the bed that people should not be in together, and we are dealing with the things that they should not be doing in that bed but are. But this verse does not just speak of a *defiled* bed; it also speaks of the *undefiled bed,* which is that pure union between the main beams of the home, the man and his wife.

There are many pieces of furniture in the home. Almost every home has a dining room table, for instance. But very few homes ever break up over the dining room table. Almost every home has a couch. But very few homes break up over the couch, unless the husband spends a lot of time sleeping on it. Almost every home has a dresser or two, but homes don't normally break up over dressers. But every home has a bed, and homes by the tens of thousands, every single year, break up over that bed. More to the point, they break up over what does or does not happen in that bed. And this is not just non-Christians homes we're talking about. Christian homes break up as often or more often than non-Christian homes over the issue of intimacy. I have been in churches where every message was a soul-winning message, every service. Lots of people got saved, but the church reached a plateau that it could never get by, mostly because so many of those homes ended up breaking up, because the home was never preached on. It was always about winning new converts.

What is so sad about that is that God Himself created sex, God Himself gave it as a gift to man and wife, and God Himself wrote enough about it in His Word to keep homes from falling apart over it if they would only obey what His Word teaches. So for the next few moments, let us go where angels fear to tread and find out what the undefiled bed must be.

The undefiled bed must be:

A culmination of an affectionate day.

2 Timothy 3:1 *This know also, that in the last days perilous times shall come. 2 For men shall be lovers of their own selves, covetous, boasters, proud, blasphemers, disobedient to parents, unthankful, unholy, 3 Without natural affection.*

As Paul came upon the last days of his life, he wrote a letter to a young preacher named Timothy. He spoke to him of many things, including what things would be like in the last days, *our days.* One mark of the last days is that people are without *natural affection.* That term means that people do no behave sociably toward each other, and they do not cherish those they claim to love. Oh how accurately that describes our day! When Susan Smith can push her car into the dark waters of a South Carolina pond, and then walk away while her little boys are screaming for mercy, we have truly reached a time when people are without natural affection. When Fox News carries a different missing person/family murder scandal every night, people are without natural affection.

That disturbing trend plays a large roll in the problems that many Christian homes are experiencing in the bedroom. Let me explain:

Men and women, as we have repeatedly said, are very different in many ways, including what it normally takes to prepare them properly for the act of intimacy. Truthfully, men really do like for a woman to be affectionate with them leading up to intimacy, but it is

89

really not necessary. All that is normally necessary for a man to be ready for intimacy is an attractive sight. For instance, in verse two of II Samuel 12, David *sees* an attractive woman, Bathsheba, and two verses later he is sleeping with her. She didn't send him flowers, or write him notes, or fix him a meal; she just looked good. Ladies, your husband enjoys affection leading up to intimacy, but if you keep yourself looking good for him, he will probably enjoy intimacy with or without it.

Ladies, though, are very different. Ladies, do you know when sex begins, in a man's mind? When the clothes start coming off, it has begun.

Men, do you know when sex begins in a lady's mind? From the very first interaction you have when you wake up in the morning. Wise men know this. Look with me at the Song of Solomon 2:8-17. Pay attention to two things: one, how this man woos this women, showering her with affection. Two, how the bedroom isn't even involved in his affection for her:

Song of Solomon 2:8 *The voice of my beloved! behold, he cometh leaping upon the mountains, skipping upon the hills. 9 My beloved is like a roe or a young hart: behold, he standeth behind our wall, he looketh forth at the windows, shewing himself through the lattice. 10 My beloved spake, and said unto me, Rise up, my love, my fair one, and come away. 11 For, lo, the winter is past, the rain is over and gone; 12 The flowers appear on the earth; the time of the singing of birds is come, and the voice of the turtle is heard in our land; 13 The fig tree putteth forth her green figs, and the vines with the tender grape give a good smell. Arise, my love, my fair one, and come away. 14 O my dove, that art in the clefts of the rock, in the secret places of the stairs, let me see thy countenance, let me hear thy voice; for sweet is thy voice, and thy countenance is comely. 15 Take us the foxes, the little foxes, that spoil the vines: for our vines have tender grapes. 16 My beloved is mine, and I am his: he feedeth among the lilies. 17 Until the day break, and the shadows flee away, turn, my beloved, and be thou like a roe or a young hart upon the mountains of Bether.*

Talk about affection! Talk about romance! He is making her heart turn flips with the affection he is showering her with, but he hasn't even suggested that he and his dear spouse head for the bedroom! Is he crazy? Is he gay? No, this man knows what it takes to make a woman want to head for the bedroom. Look at the next four verses:

Song of Solomon 3:1 *By night on my bed I sought him whom my soul loveth: I sought him, but I found him not. 2 I will rise now, and go about the city in the streets, and in the broad ways I will seek him whom my soul loveth: I sought him, but I found him not. 3 The watchmen that go about the city found me: to whom I said, Saw ye him whom my soul loveth? 4 It was but a little that I passed from them, but I found him whom my soul loveth: I held him, and would not let him go, until I had brought him into my mother's house, and into the chamber of her that conceived me.*

Men, did you understand all this? This man showed this woman with affection, and she dragged him into the bedroom. MMMM, can I get a witness!

The undefiled bed needs to be the culmination of an affectionate day. Men, from your first day of marriage till death do you part, you need to shower your wife with affection. You need to kiss that woman early and often, hold her hand, hug her repeatedly, call her just to hear her voice, write her love letters, send flowers, whisper sweet things in her ear, open doors for her, give her romantic glances, her cup of affection needs to run over on a daily basis. One of my favorite phrases that God has ever given me is this:

If you treat her right when the sun is up high, she'll treat you right when the moon's in the sky.

The undefiled bed must be the culmination of an affectionate day! It must also be:

A constant source of enjoyment.

Proverbs 5:18 *Let thy fountain be blessed: and rejoice with the wife of thy youth. 19 Let her be as the loving hind and pleasant roe; let* *her breasts satisfy thee at all times; and be thou ravished always with her love.*

It is very obvious from these verse and the verses around them that what is being discussed is the physical act of love, intimacy, sexuality. God, in the book of the Bible dedicated to wisdom, gave wise words on the undefiled bed. He said, specifically, that a man is to be *ravished always* with the sexual love of his wife.

I would like to be a help here, and I hope I am able to help you more than I was able to help another young couple. I preached on the home at my church, and dealt with this passage. When I explained what it meant, a young Bible college couple was there. He looked like he was hearing the very words of God from heaven. She looked like she was hearing the cursing of Satan from hell! She went back to the college president and told him that I was "obsessed with sex!" She demanded to her husband that they leave the church, and he obediently followed. As far as I can tell, that boy is still a poor starving soul, wondering what in the world he has gotten into. Please don't do that, listen carefully to what God's Word says, and it will help you.

This word *ravished* is the Hebrew word *shawgah,* and it literally means to be absolutely intoxicated with something, to stagger, reel, and roll! The word "always" simply means "always." The picture is that of someone who stays falling down drunk for years and years and years, and never even sobers up.

Perhaps you wonder how in the world that picture applies to the bedroom. Here's how: Ladies, were you with me when I told your husbands they need to be affectionate, send flowers, etc? Are you still with me? Please stay with me then, because it is your husband's turn to shout the victory.

Here is what God is saying: just like a drunk drinks and drinks and drinks and then drinks some more, you need to be in bed and in bed and in bed (awake, together) more and more and more and more. You can't get drunk off a little sip now and then. Ladies, it is your job to get your husband stoned slap drunk on your love.

My wife was looking for TV news early one morning, and came across Dr. Phil. He was talking to young couples about to marry. He had asked the man how often they would want to have sex. He answered... "Well, a bunch." He asked her the same question, and she answered, "Never, I'll just be happy to be married." I shot straight up in bed and screamed at that boy on TV, "RUN! RUN FOR YOUR LIFE!"

Ladies, in general, men have a greater sexual appetite than you do. It is the one who is hungry that will be prone to go out looking for snacks, so you better be sure to never let him get hungry. The undefiled bed must be a constant source of enjoyment. But it must also be:

A challenge to the world's temptations.

Men and women, but women especially, may I show you from God's Word what your spouse is up against in this wicked world?

Proverbs 7:1 *My son, keep my words, and lay up my commandments with thee. 2 Keep my commandments, and live; and my law as the apple of thine eye. 3 Bind them upon thy fingers, write them upon the table of thine heart. 4 Say unto wisdom, Thou art my sister; and call understanding thy kinswoman: 5 That they may keep thee from the strange woman, from the stranger which flattereth with her words. 6 For at the window of my house I looked through my casement, 7 And beheld among the simple ones, I discerned among the youths, a young man void of understanding, 8 Passing through the street near her corner; and he went the way to her house, 9 In the twilight, in the evening, in the black and dark night: 10 And, behold, there met him a woman with the attire of an harlot, and subtil of heart. 11 (She is loud and stubborn; her feet abide not in her house: 12 Now is she without, now in the streets, and lieth in wait at every corner.) 13 So she caught him, and kissed him, and with an impudent face said unto him, 14 I have peace offerings with me; this day have I payed my vows. 15 Therefore came I forth to meet thee, diligently to seek thy face, and I have found thee. 16 I have decked my bed with coverings of* *tapestry, with carved works, with fine linen of Egypt. 17 I have perfumed my bed with myrrh, aloes, and cinnamon. 18 Come, let us take our fill of love until the morning: let us solace ourselves with loves. 19 For the goodman is not at home, he is gone a long journey: 20 He hath taken a bag of money with him, and will come home at the day appointed. 21 With her much fair speech she caused him to yield, with the flattering of her lips she forced him.*

Welcome to America, twenty-first century. This man is out and about, and a woman spots him. She is attractive, she is immodestly dressed, she is seductive, she is sexually aggressive, she has a neat, clean bedroom just waiting, she is offering not one, but multiple encounters (notice that "loves" in verse 18 is plural) and she is great at flattery. This guy falls and falls hard.

The devil knows exactly what attracts your mate. And whether you like it or not, he will do his best to steal your husband or wife from you. He will use the most attractive bait he can find, and if you are not careful, you will lose your spouse. Everywhere you go today there are pictures and posters of immodest men and women. You can no longer walk down the street without half of the people you meet being dressed in such a way that it catches your eye. Every commercial and billboard and newspaper and magazine lures your spouse towards evil. That is the bad news. Would you like the good news? The good news is this; right now, you are holding a hand full of aces, and you can play them every day. You're holding most all of the cards. You are married. Your spouse thought you were attractive, or he or she wouldn't have married you to start with. You can give your spouse rightly what others are luring him or her to take wrongly. The problem is, most people act as if the battle is already won, and they don't even have to compete anymore.

You can feel and act that way if you want to, and you will most likely end up as another shocking divorce statistic.

(Do you understand that the devil will try to lure your mate away? What are you going to do about it?)

The undefiled must be a challenge to the world's temptations. Ladies, you have got to fight for your man. From the pulpit to the pew, you have got to fight for your man. You absolutely must use the bed and body that God has given you to make your spouse temptation proof. You absolutely must use the bed and body that God has given you to make your spouse not desire to look on another woman in lust. The undefiled must be a challenge to the world's temptations. It must also be:

A creative field of imagination.

How many of you have ever heard the ten commandments of marital sexuality? Let me give them to you:

a.   Thou shalt not be boring
b.   Thou shalt not be boring
c.   Thou shalt not be boring
d.   Thou shalt not be boring
e.   Thou shalt not be boring
f.   Thou shalt not be boring
g.   Thou shalt not be boring
h.   Thou shalt not be boring
i.   Thou shalt not be boring
j.   Thou really really shalt not be boring

"Preacher you made them up!" No, I just paraphrased a Biblical principle: **Genesis 26:8** *And it came to pass, when he had been there a long time, that Abimelech king of the Philistines looked out at a window, and saw, and, behold, Isaac was sporting with Rebekah his wife.*

Golf was invented in about 1200 A.D. Basketball is just over a hundred years old. Baseball is about 200 years old. Isaac and Rebekah were married about 3500 years ago. They were not playing golf, or basketball, or football, or soccer, or cricket, or tennis, or any other modern sport. But they were playing. That word *sporting* is the Hebrew word *tsawchak.* It indicates to play sexually, and one of its primary definitions is *to make a toy of another!* These two got real,

95

real creative. Maybe a little too creative, being as how someone else managed to see them! You say "Preacher, that is awful!" Yes, I agree. But it's obvious they didn't mean to be seen, so I'm willing to cut them some slack. But do you know what is really awful? People that are so very careful and reserved and boring and dull that their marriage dies a slow, silent death. Friends, for all of Isaac and Rebekah's faults, they at least got this right; their undefiled bed was a bed of creativity, and intrigue, and excitement. I mean, when the king catches you at it, you are living life on the edge!

God did not make sex just for procreation, but also for recreation. Remember that bit about being *ravished always* with her love?

In the large church I grew up in, ladies meetings were held monthly. There was a nice old couple in the church, late sixties, who never had any children. The pastor's wife asked her to speak at one of the ladies meetings. She did so. My wife came and told me how informative it was. For instance, she was informed by this lady that lingerie was of the devil, and that a wife should never dress provocatively at home for her husband. Wearing such things would incite lustful passions and make him behave in an inappropriate manner. The ladies were further informed that sex was only for procreation, never for recreation. The next speaker at the ladies meeting was the pastor, undoing the damage that woman did!

The undefiled bed must be a creative field of imagination. Truthfully, when you are married adults, cops and robbers is a lot more fun than it was as kids! Same thing for cowboys and Indians, and doctor, and strange foreigner, and master and maid, and just about anything else! Go ahead and get mad if you want to, but your spouse is hoping you're paying attention.

The undefiled bed must also be:

A completed act for both.

I am going to be very careful at this point in the words I use, so that adults will understand perfectly, and little eyes will be oblivious.

Philippians 2:3 *Let nothing be done through strife or vainglory; but in lowliness of mind let each esteem other better than themselves. 4 Look not every man on his own things, but every man also on the things of others.*

Don't think for a moment I have read the wrong verse here. It's the right one for what I am saying. In everything, we are to regard others better than ourselves. In everything, we are to make sure that things go well for others as well as for ourselves. Nowhere is this more true than in the home, and especially in the bedroom.

A young lady came to my wife for counseling after more than a decade of marriage. As far as she was concerned, things were over. It turns out that she and her husband were in the bedroom really, really often, but that in more than a decade, the husband had only taken care of her needs twice. When he was satisfied, they were done. Well congratulations, sir, now you two really are done.

Men, the ladies have been troopers so far through this book. We have told them to get you drunk on their love, and be creative, and fight for you in bed. Now it is your turn to hear some things you might not like to hear.

If you are going through life, in bed, being satisfied but not satisfying your spouse, you are violating Philippians 2:3-4. Maybe you don't yet know how to accomplish what your wife needs. Then let me recommend a book. It is written by a Christian man and wife, who also happen to both be medical doctors. It is called Intended For Pleasure, by Ed and Gaye Wheate. You can find everything you need to know there. Men, not only do you need to satisfy your wife, you need to consider many times satisfying her first. Your wife is just as capable of being lured away as you are.

In addition to all of these things, be sure that the undefiled bed is also:

A Christ centered activity.
1 Corinthians 10:31 *Whether therefore ye eat, or drink, or whatsoever ye do, do all to the glory of God.*

97

Colossians 1:18 *And he is the head of the body, the church: who is the beginning, the firstborn from the dead; that in all things he might have the preeminence.*

As I finish the twelve weeks of marriage counseling that I put all married-couples-to-be through at our church, I end with a lesson teaching the couple to put Christ at the center of all things. Christ must be at the center of your finances, and child rearing, and education, and activities, and jobs, and He must be at the center of the undefiled bed. Your love life with your spouse is not just for his or her pleasure; it is also for God's glory. He must have the preeminence in it. If He does, you will forgive your spouse for his or her wrongs, like Christ has forgiven you, and you will not hold those wrongs against your spouse in the bedroom. If He has the preeminence, then the one with the lesser appetite will not hesitate to fulfill the one with the greater appetite. If He has the preeminence, then a husband will shower his wife with affection before he ever expects intimacy. If He has the preeminence, then you will use the undefiled bed to fight for your spouse, and to make him or her less susceptible to the temptations the world is going to present. If He has the preeminence, then you will not allow things to get boring. If He has the preeminence, then you will ensure that both end up satisfied.

But as we close this chapter, understand this: If He has the preeminence, then even if things do not go as you want them to in the bedroom, you will still love your spouse, you will still be faithful, you will still be true, because that is how God loves us, even when we disappoint Him. He never uses our failures as an excuse to do wrong Himself.

Ladies and gentleman, main beams of the home, there is no more important piece of furniture in your home than the undefiled bed.

PART EIGHT:
PREPARING FOR A RAINY DAY

True story: A man thought he had conquered the problem of trying to remember his wife's birthday and their anniversary. So he opened an account with a florist, provided him with the dates and instructions to send flowers along with an appropriate note signed, "Your loving husband." That worked out really well... until one day when he came home, kissed his wife and said offhandedly, "Nice flowers, honey. Where'd you get them?"

After we got the beams for the building up, we turned our attention to putting up "R-Panels." R-Panels are the sheets of metal that cover every wall and the entire roof. There is one, and only one reason to do that: Rain! If it never rained, we would have made an open-air tabernacle, and saved a lot of time and money. But it does rain. We don't know when it is going to rain, we don't know how light or heavy it will be, so we just prepare for the worst and make the entire building rainproof. We put gutters on it, we put down-spout drains that go 50-100 feet away from the building. All of that was in preparation for a rainy day.

When we speak of "preparing for a rainy day" in regards to the home, you know that we are talking about money, about doing what is necessary to prepare for any hard days ahead.

99

Let me put it another way: you may not be able to buy happiness by handling money wisely, but you can surely buy unhappiness by handling it unwisely!

The week that I was studying for the message that produced this chapter of the book, my wife looked over at me and asked me what I was preaching on. I told her that the message would be on money, and then I reminded her of the statistics that point to money as the number one source of divorce. The very next day while riding together in the car, a USA radio news report said the very same thing! Then they went a step further, and quickly offered a few solutions... all of which were terrible. It is a shame to think that people will follow bad monetary advice, especially when God's Word will tell you most everything you need to know.

So let's look into God's Word, and learn how to help our homes by preparing for a rainy day.

First and foremost, remember that everything belongs to God.

Exodus 19:5 *Now therefore, if ye will obey my voice indeed, and keep my covenant, then ye shall be a peculiar treasure unto me above all people: for all the earth is mine.*

Psalm 50:12 *If I were hungry, I would not tell thee: for the world is mine, and the fulness thereof.*

This principle will not only come as a surprise to many lost people, but to a great number of Christians as well! Many Christians believe that a tenth of what we earn belongs to God. That estimate is ninety per cent too low. The land that you have your name on belongs to God. The home that you hold a title deed to belongs to God. The person that you married belongs to God. The cars that you are driving belong to God. When we realize that, it makes perfect sense to use God's Word as our financial guide.

Now, a word of caution should be inserted at this point: the Pentecostal/Charismatic movement often takes this principle, and then perverts it. They teach that "Since God owns it all, and since we are His children, He obviously intends for us all to be wealthy. And if you aren't driving the nicest cars, and wearing designer clothes, and living in a mansion, you must not have much faith!" Don't believe me? Listen to these examples:

A Word Faith teacher named David Epley sent out a brochure along with a bar of "prayer blessed soap." The brochure claimed that, "We are going to wash away all BAD LUCK, SICKNESS, MISFORTUNES and EVIL." Inside the brochure was a personal letter from Epley with a full page of instructions on how to use the soap for healing or a "money miracle." He said "Now, after you wash the poverty from your hands, take out the largest bill or check you have... that $100, $50, or $20 bill... hold it in your clean hands and say "In Jesus name I dedicate this gift to God's work... and expect a miracle in the return of money." Epley then conveniently provided the address of his own organization to send that "clean money" to!

Word Faith Publications include these titles, "How to Write Your Own Ticket With God," "Godliness is Profitable," "The Laws of Prosperity," "God's Formula for Success and Prosperity," "God's Master Key to Prosperity," and "Living in Divine Prosperity." Clearly, money is big with the Charismatic movement! Remember the PTL and Jim Baker? Creflo Dollar, another prominent Charismatic with an appropriate last name often claims that, "Jesus wore the finest of clothes, He was a fashion plate, and He expects us to have the finest as well!" This despite the fact that Jesus said in Matthew 8:20 "The foxes have holes, and the birds of the air have nests; but the Son of man hath not where to lay his head."

So apparently, Jesus didn't have much faith.

No, the truth is, God does own it all, and He often blesses us, but He owes us nothing, and we owe Him everything.

Obey God in tithes and offerings from your earliest days, and make sure you marry someone who feels the same way.

You would not believe the amount of times I have counseled with Christian couples who were having awful arguments about whether or not to obey God in this matter!

Let me just remind you of a few verses, and then make a few specific applications:

Malachi 3:8 *Will a man rob God? Yet ye have robbed me. But ye say, Wherein have we robbed thee? In tithes and offerings. 9 Ye are cursed with a curse: for ye have robbed me, even this whole nation. 10 Bring ye all the tithes into the storehouse, that there may be meat in mine house, and prove me now herewith, saith the LORD of hosts, if I will not open you the windows of heaven, and pour you out a blessing, that there shall not be room enough to receive it.*

Genesis 14:18 *And Melchizedek king of Salem brought forth bread and wine: and he was the priest of the most high God. 19 And he blessed him, and said, Blessed be Abram of the most high God, possessor of heaven and earth: 20 And blessed be the most high God, which hath delivered thine enemies into thy hand. And he gave him tithes of all.*

Hebrews 7:1 *For this Melchisedec, king of Salem, priest of the most high God, who met Abraham returning from the slaughter of the kings, and blessed him; 2 To whom also Abraham gave a tenth part of all; first being by interpretation King of righteousness, and after that also King of Salem, which is, King of peace;*

Proverbs 3:9 *Honour the LORD with thy substance, and with the firstfruits of all thine increase: 10 So shall thy barns be filled with plenty, and thy presses shall burst out with new wine.*

And here is a small list of the verses where God speaks of giving freewill gifts above the tithes as God has blessed you: Leviticus 22:18, 21, 23; Leviticus 23:38; Numbers 15:3; Numbers 29:39; Deuteronomy 12:6, 17; Deuteronomy 16:10 Deuteronomy 23:23; II Chronicles 31:14; Ezra 1:4; Ezra 3:5; Ezra 7:16; Ezra 8:28

God's Word is abundantly clear on this: We owe God a tenth of our gross, and then we give a freewill offering above that because we love Him.

Here is how that applies to marriage, to the home, and here is how it helps us to prepare for a rainy day:

God has promised to bless tithers, as we saw in Malachi 3:8-10.

He didn't say He would make us filthy rich, but He did promise to bless us. And He also promised to fight against us if we disobey Him. It is really hard to get ahead when God is fighting against us.

If you can rob God and not have Him fight against you, you are lost. God doesn't care if lost people give or not. This is all about His relationship with His children. His children know, or will learn the hard way, not to rob Him. Lots of saved couples have their tithe taken out by the mechanic. Lots of saved couples have their tithe taken out by the doctor. Lots of saved couples have their tithe taken out by the taxman. Lots of saved couples have their tithe taken out by the home repairman. Lots of saved couples have their tithe taken out by the dentist or orthodontist. It is hard to avoid fights in marriage when God is chastening your checkbook!

If you cannot agree on something so basic and simple, you will find that you disagree about lots of other things as well.

I have never, never, never counseled a couple that was arguing about tithing that was not also arguing about other things! Listen to me: tithing is good for your home!

One of the nicest things for a couple is to look at the statement at the end of the year, and realize how much they have done together during the year for the Lord. You know these things, so let's hasten on.

When you start working, start investing.

Let me ask you a few easy questions: Will it be easier to find a good spouse if you are penniless, or fairly well off?

Will a home be more likely to struggle if you are broke, or fairly well off?

How about this: is being wealthy a sin?

How about this simple question: if it were fairly easy to become rich, at least by the time you retire, would you like to know how?

Now let me show you something:

Proverbs 6:6 *Go to the ant, thou sluggard; consider her ways, and be wise:* **7** *Which having no guide, overseer, or ruler,* **8** *Provideth her meat in the summer, and gathereth her food in the harvest.*

Summer is the earlier part of the year. The ant prepares for the winter months before the winter ever arrives, and God calls her wise for doing so.

If you want to do it, young people, becoming wealthy will be a fairly easy thing for you. Let me explain how. You don't have to get lucky, you don't have to become a pro athlete, or get a recording contract. Nope, all you have to do is experience the magic of compound interest. Let me show you how it works.

Let's take Jessica, 16. Jessica, at 16 years old, starts putting $25.00 a week into a mutual fund. It comes out of her check pre-tax, so she has automatically saved about 20% on it. Then, all of the interest it accumulates is also tax deferred every single year.

The stock market has up years and down years, but over the long-term average it produces about a ten percent return per year. Jessica is putting $25.00 per week into her account. That doesn't sound like much, but she does it every year till she is 20. Then she ups it to $50.00 per week. Still doesn't seem like much, but she does it faithfully, every year till age 60. Give me a guess at the small sums of $25.00 per week for those first four years, and $50.00 per week for the next forty, how much will she have put into her account? $109,200.

I am betting that a lot of you are thinking, "Man! I wish I was going to have that much money when I retire!"

I didn't say that is how much she would have; I said it is how much she was going to have put in. Do you have any idea how much she will have? $1,566,183.48.

Get that! She put in a measly $25.00 per week instead of buying ipods or sodas or pizzas. Then when she got twenty, she put in a puny $50.00 per week by buying a used car for cash instead of a new one. And without even really trying hard, she finds herself at 60 years old with more than a million and a half dollars! Oh by the way, if she left that money in that account for another seven years, which is pretty standard now, to not touch retirement money till age 67, by that time she would have $3,052,047!

You say you can't afford to invest? I say you can't afford not to! There will be a lot of people who get to retirement age, and find themselves working minimum wage jobs to make ends meet. But if young people will invest early and wisely, they most likely wont have to do that. You can spend your golden years with money to give to God's work, money to go on cruises, money for a huge house, money to take care of your elderly parents (and maybe money to be a blessing to your old preacher! Just a thought...).

What is the key? Starting early, like the ant, and doing it consistently for the rest of your life. So many college age kids are thrilled just to have a checking account in their name. I say, by the time you are in college, you should have a mutual fund in your name with a decent amount in it!

Couples, if you haven't started investing yet, you should sit down with your budget, and find out ways to make it happen. If you work for a company that has any kind of matching fund retirement plan, take advantage of it! If you don't, you are giving away free money!

I used to work for a company that would put .50 in for every dollar I put in up to 6%. I made about $300.00 per week at the time. Some guys said, "I'm not putting 6% of my money into some account!" I said "I'm not leaving $9.00 per week in my boss's account when I can make him put it in my account instead!"

We could go on about this forever, but just trust me: from the earliest days, start investing for the future! One day your future spouse will thank you. When he or she does, just say "Don't thank me, thank Dr. Wagner..."

Live on a budget instead of flying blind!

Luke 14:28 *For Which of you, intending to build a tower, sitteth not down first, and counteth the cost, whether he have sufficient to finish it?* **29** *Lest haply, after he hath laid the foundation, and is not able to finish it, all that behold it begin to mock him,* **30** *Saying, This man began to build, and was not able to finish.*

The practical side of this passage teaches the foolishness of not having a budget. Jesus said these words. The same Jesus who died on Calvary for us took time to tell us to learn to budget! Every child should be taught by their parents how to budget. Every couple should present a working budget before a pastor will consent to marry them. I am not trying to be mean, but a preacher who will marry a young couple without ever checking into their budgeting skills is either lazy or careless. This is too important to trust to chance!

A budget doesn't have to be rocket science. It doesn't have to be on a spreadsheet. Simply put, you need to begin by putting on paper what you make, not including overtime. (It comes and goes, and therefore cannot be counted on. Make that extra saving money).

By the way, it is also very helpful not to include a young wife's salary in the budget numbers (again, use that for extra saving money). Why is that? Because young wives tend to get pregnant. If you have lived on just the husband's salary, the wife will be able to quit and stay home with the babies if you choose. But if you have lived to the max on both your salary and hers, you will be hurting bad when the doctor puts her on bed rest! You will be hurting worse when she tells you that the desire of her heart is to stay home with her own babies and be a full time stay at home mom to them.

So begin by putting your income down. Then subtract the tithe and offerings, then the savings both long term and short term. Then whatever you have left is what you can live on, so get a home and vehicles and everything else that will fit into what you have. It is called "living within your means." If you do that from your first job for the rest of your life, from the first day of marriage for the rest of your life, you will have a relatively stress free life!

Some of you are already married, and some of you are thinking, "I wish I'd heard this years ago." It's not too late. Get out that piece of paper, and get to work.

We are not to be greedy of or hasty for wealth - Proverbs 28:20-22, 23:5.

I've already pointed out that wealth is not a sin, and that investing early and consistently can make you wealthy. But that is very different from greed or being hasty (in a hurry) for wealth:

Proverbs 28:20 *A faithful man shall abound with blessings: but he that maketh haste to be rich shall not be innocent.* *21* *To have respect of persons is not good: for for a piece of bread that man will transgress.* *22* *He that hasteth to be rich hath an evil eye, and considereth not that poverty shall come upon him.*

Proverbs 23:5 *Wilt thou set thine eyes upon that which is not? for riches certainly make themselves wings; they fly away as an eagle toward heaven.*

Greed of and haste for wealth will take different forms, but the more common ones are these:

Gambling (lottery tickets, video poker, etc.)

Theft

Pyramid Schemes

These things have ruined homes and lives! And they are all signs that money has become your God.

We are to be fearful of debt.

Proverbs 22:7 *The rich ruleth over the poor, and the borrower is servant to the lender.*

Debt is not necessarily a sin, but it is rarely a good idea, and it is something that we should have a healthy fear of.

This is especially true of debt for items that depreciate. What does it mean for something to depreciate? To go down in value. What are some examples of things that depreciate? TV's, cars, clothes, food, electronics, furniture. Basically, almost anything other than a home or property will probably depreciate in value.

So when a person goes into debt for a depreciating item, they will at some point be paying more for that item than it is worth.

This is especially true for credit card debt. Who are credit cards designed to benefit? Credit cards are designed for the benefit of the *credit card companies*, not for your benefit. No person ever said, "You know, I think I'd like to be a real help to millions of Americans. I think I'll start a credit card company."

Late fees are enormous. If you miss a payment on a $50.00 item, you will pay a $29.00 late fee in a single month!

Most credit card companies have their main offices in states that have no legal cap on credit card interest rates. Rates can go up, literally, to any amount they want, at any time. That is a ticking time bomb waiting to blow up. Fear debt, especially credit card debt. This will reduce stress in marriages. It will free people up to give. It is one of the most valuable things you can do for your finances.

No, it's not a sin to have a credit card. But just like a gun, you have to be very careful with it, or it may be you or your family that you kill with it!

We are not to be lazy or wasteful.

Proverbs 18:9 *He also that is slothful in his work is brother to him that is a great waster.*

In counseling people financially, we will deal with both their outgo and their income. This verse deals with both. A lazy person will not *make* much; a wasteful person will not *keep* much.

A lady called my church, asking for help with her rent. She was about $90.00 short each month being able to pay it. In the middle of her plea, she said "excuse me for a minute while I light up this cigarette." Then she finished asking for help from my church. I told her I would be glad to help her. I asked her how many packs of cigarettes she smoked a day. Two. I did some quick figuring on an adding machine, and told her I had her problem solved. All she had to do was quit smoking, and she would have enough money for the rent each month with some to spare. She hung up. How rude.

Laziness is a sin. Wastefulness is a sin. And either of them will kill a budget.

Please don't misunderstand me. I am not saying you should go into "Kernels in the freezer mode." What is that, you ask? I went into my grandmother's freezer for some ice some years ago, and came across a zip-loc bag with exactly three kernels of corn in it...

Don't go there, ok? But don't be wasteful or lazy, either. And don't marry anyone who is lazy or wasteful. Especially you girls, don't ever marry some sorry, low-life, lazy loser! It is a hard thing for a girl to find herself having to work two jobs to support her dead-beat husband.

We are to plan and think long term.

1 Timothy 5:8 *But if any provide not for his own, and specially for those of his own house, he hath denied the faith, and is worse than an infidel.*

This word *provide* speaks of seeing a need, even a need far off, and meeting that need before it arrives. Here are some simple things based on this verse.

Have your house paid off well before you retire. One of the saddest things I ever see is couples in their sixties and seventies with a thirty year mortgage stretching out in front of them, and I see it a lot.

The husband (at least) should have a life insurance policy. Especially for a Christian, this is an excellent idea. Why? Because we do not smoke, drink, or do drugs, we get preferred rates! It is not at all uncommon to secure a half-million dollar policy for $40-$50 a month. This will provide for our families even after we are gone.

By the way, if you are smart enough to begin an IRA early, then your life insurance should be annual renewable term. It is vastly cheaper than whole life, and by the time you have been investing in a mutual fund IRA for a few decades, you will not even need the life insurance policy if you do not want it.

Be sure to enjoy with gladness the fruit of your labors.

Acts 2:46 *And they, continuing daily with one accord in the temple, and breaking bread from house to house, **did eat their meat with gladness and singleness of heart,***

This may sound odd, but trust me, it's another thing I see a good bit of. There are some folks who actually do quite well with money. They tithe, they save, they live within their means.... and they are miserable because they never do anything to enjoy all of that hard work and saving and tithing and budgeting.

Dana's grandparents had several hundred thousand dollars. Yet they lived like misers, they never went on vacation, they never left Andalusia, Alabama, they never saw the world. All their meals were at home. There were no dates. They grew old, they clung tightly to their money... and then they got old enough for the government to take it all so they could go to the nursing home and let Medicaid pay for it. That is a really bad plan.

I don't want to get to the end of my life going, *"Ehh, I beat 'em all. I ate crackers and drank water at home while they went to the Outback. I worked overtime while they went on vacation. I married my wife, and then never took her on another date. I used dial up internet! Ehh heh heh. Yep, I saved every dime, and never had a single ounce of fun, and that's why I'm wearing a much better quality of adult diaper than that poor sap across the hall from me..."*

The rainy day is coming... how prepared are you?

PART NINE:
" I" IS FOR INSULATION

A business man's wife was experiencing depression. She began to mope around and be sad, lifeless – no light in her eyes – no spring in her step – joyless. It became so bad that this "man of the world" did what any sophisticated person would do. He made an appointment with the psychiatrist. They went to the psychiatrist's office, sat down with him and began to talk. It wasn't long before the wise doctor realized what the problem was. So, without saying a word, he simply stood, walked over in front of the woman's chair, signaled her to stand, took her by the hands, then gathered her into his arms and gave her a big, warm hug, then a long, passionate kiss. You could see the change come over the woman. Her face softened, her eyes lit up, she immediately relaxed. Her whole face glowed. Stepping back, the doctor said to the husband, "See, that's all she needs." With that, the man said, "Okay, I'll bring her in Tuesdays and Thursdays each week, but I have to play golf on the other afternoons."

In our new church building, in a few months, people will be walking in and sitting down and fellowshipping and listening to preaching. They will do so in the winter, yet they will be warm and comfortable. They will do so in the summer, yet they will be cool and comfortable. Yet the reason for this won't even be seen. Hidden in every single wall cavity, there is roll after roll of scratchy, itchy, dry, horrible tasting insulation. I have coughed and hacked and wheezed my way through the last year, mostly because we have put around 800 roles of insulation in that building.

Why did we do this? Why did we subject ourselves to such torture? *So that we could control the atmosphere in the building.* We don't want it too hot, we don't want it too cold, and we don't want sound bleeding over from one room into the next.

Oh how well this applies to the home!

Have you ever paid attention to the fact that every home has it's own "atmosphere" that is produced by the people within the home?

Some homes are laid back and enjoyable...

Some homes are dignified and formal...

Some homes are so stuffy and sterile you may as well be in a museum...

Some homes are cold as ice...

Some homes are harsh, angry, almost open warfare...

Every home has it's own atmosphere. If the atmosphere isn't right, no one will be comfortable. That is where the "I" in Insulation comes in.

"I" will honestly evaluate whether those around me enjoy being in my home.

1 Thessalonians 5:21 *Prove all things; hold fast that which is good.*

This verse isn't just for doctrine; it is also for behavior! This goes for dads, moms, and kids. People either enjoy the atmosphere you are helping to produce in the home, or they don't. Obviously, it applies most to the adults, for you do the most to set the atmosphere in the home.

Some of you are married, but don't have kids yet. How is the atmosphere in your home?

Some of you are parents. How is the atmosphere in your home? I would wager to say that a lot of people have never even

112

given this much conscious thought. They give thought to the yard that needs mowing, the dishes that need doing, but no thought at all to whether people are happy or miserable in their home.

Let me once again insert a word of warning here, especially to the young people: when your parents run the home Biblically, I can promise you there will be some things about it your flesh doesn't like. Get over it. You may think that a 1:00 a.m. curfew would improve the atmosphere in your home. You are sadly mistaken, so just get over it and move on.

But as we begin this chapter, let's begin it here. Honestly evaluate whether your family enjoys or endures the atmosphere you help to produce in your home.

You may want to ask your spouse about this. You may be blissfully unaware. If you ask, promise ahead of time that you will not get mad if you hear something you don't like, otherwise you may not get a totally honest answer.

"I" will refrain from criticizing and belittling within the walls of my home.

2 Samuel 6:20 *Then David returned to bless his household. And Michal the daughter of Saul came out to meet David, and said, How glorious was the king of Israel to day, who uncovered himself to day in the eyes of the handmaids of his servants, as one of the vain fellows shamelessly uncovereth himself!*

One of the best ways to produce a poison atmosphere in the home is criticism and belittling, as demonstrated in this passage.

If you think you can call your spouse names and produce a good atmosphere, or have him/her conform to what you want, think again.

A guy I used to go to church with had a wife that was way too pretty for him. He knew it. So he beat her down verbally, calling her fatty, and many other things. Well, his home is a lot quieter today. That tends to happen when your spouse walks away forever.

A lady I used to work with beat her husband to death with her mouth, all, day every day. Truthfully, he had an awesome spirit, and could have been something special. She ruined him, and their marriage.

The same thing is true of children. Build them up, don't tear them down. Refrain from criticizing others as well, for this is where most criticizing spirits are learned, and copied.

The good atmosphere of a home will make neighborhood kids come over and play, your pet puppy dog want to stay, and grumbling whiners stay away!

PART TEN:
SURE I HAVE A SECURITY SYSTEM; THAT
SCREEN DOOR IS TOP OF THE LINE!

L et me tell you "The Perfect Story:" There was a perfect man who met a perfect woman. After a perfect courtship, they had a perfect wedding. Their life together was, of course, perfect.

One snowy, stormy Christmas Eve this perfect couple was driving along a winding road when they noticed someone at the roadside in distress. Being the perfect couple, they stopped to help. There stood Santa Claus with a huge bundle of toys. Not wanting to disappoint any children on the eve of Christmas, the perfect couple loaded Santa and his toys into their vehicle. Soon they were driving along delivering the toys. Unfortunately, the driving conditions deteriorated and the perfect couple and Santa Claus had an accident. Only one of them survived the accident. Who was the survivor?

Woman's Answer: It's obvious. The perfect woman. She's the only one that really existed in the first place, because everyone knows there is no Santa Claus and there is no such thing as a perfect man.

Man's Response: So, if there is no perfect man and no Santa Claus, the perfect woman must have been driving. This explains why there was a car accident to begin with!

When we bought our home, one of the first things we did was put in an alarm system. I am a big believer in alarm systems. We had installed, right in the hallway by our bedroom, a 90-decibel siren that would go off in case of emergency. One cold winter night when we were deeply buried beneath a mound of covers... 2:00 in the morning... *the alarm went off!* I thought I had missed the rapture. I jumped out of bed, not knowing where I was or what was going on, stubbed my toe, fumbled around for my gun, couldn't even get the drawer open where it was, ran over every piece of furniture in our bedroom, and finally got the alarm shut off. With frazzled nerves I searched every corner of the house, loaded gun ahead of me. There was no intruder anywhere. I picked up the phone to call the alarm company, and the line was dead. The ice outside had cut the phone wire. When the alarm could not communicate with central monitoring, it went off! It's a wonder I didn't shoot myself and the dog and Dana.

Still, I would not be without an alarm system. You say "but preacher, an alarm system isn't going to make a criminal stop breaking in homes." I'm not trying to get them to stop breaking in homes. I'm trying to make them pick your house instead of mine. Like the old saying goes "I don't have to outrun the grizzly bear, I just have to outrun you!" Seriously, though, every house, every business, every church should have a complete security system. Ideally you should have big strong doors with deadbolt locks, a top-notch alarm system, and a 12 gauge. Why? Because we live in a world where dangerous people do try to get in and do damage. That is why we are investing in an incredible alarm system for the new church.

Now let's apply that to the home. There are some things that are as lethal as a thug with a gun that will try to get into your home. There are some things so very dangerous you need to have a good solid spiritual security system to guard against them. I see these things wreck home after home after home. What are they, and what kind of security system can we put in place against them?

There are many dangers we could examine, in this message we will look at the "big three" home killers.

Pornography.

Psalm 101:3 *I will set no wicked thing before mine eyes: I hate the work of them that turn aside; it shall not cleave to me.*

The psalmist gave some excellent counsel in this verse. He knew that if he ever looked at anything evil, it would stick to him like glue. There has never been anything quite like pornography to stick to people's hearts, minds, and memories, and then destroy their homes. You most assuredly, if you are ever going to have a successful and stable home, need to guard against pornography at all cost.

This evil is the destroyer of some of the strongest homes you could imagine. A preacher I knew, incredible mind, good speaking skills, godly heritage, college educated, married one of the finest women the world has ever know, had a bunch of awesome and well behaved kids, lost everything because he set pornography before his eyes. He would be the first one to tell you to pay heed to this verse.

I have had wives sit in my office, bawling their eyes out over what they have found their husbands watching or looking at.

A person addicted to pornography is going to lose some things:
The affection of his wife
The respect of his children
The ability to look at a woman in the right way
The ability to have real sex with his mate

There may be many more things than these that a person addicted to pornography loses situation by situation, but all of these four are pretty much guaranteed. No good wife will tolerate having to compete with pornography for her husband's affection. She will lock him out after a while. No good children will tolerate knowing that their father has violated their mother this way. A man who succumbs to a pornography addiction will eventually view every woman in a sexual light. Whether they are church members, or strangers on the street, he will begin to look at women as sexual objects, rather than as sisters in Christ. Most shockingly, and what most men addicted to pornography do not know until it is too late, a porn addiction will eventually rob a man of the ability to have real sex with his mate.

117

Even secular counselors recognize this phenomenon. It is often called "porn creep." It is a term that means that pornography draws a man into such a realm of fantasy and unreality, that reality itself ceases to satisfy him. That is what is so insidious about people that are foolish enough to bring pornography into a marriage to "solve" problems in the bedroom. They may alleviate those problems for a while, but they will lead to a much greater problem. Pornography is lethal.

Did you realize that even the name pornography should tell you how dangerous it is? The first part of that word is from the Greek word *pornea*. It means *licentiousness, perversion, filthiness.* There is nothing on earth any filthier than pornography.

At younger and younger ages, boys especially are being exposed to this filth in our culture. Boys, young men, you shouldn't look at any picture of a woman that you would be afraid to look at if your mama were looking over your shoulder!

This is often the "hidden sin" that destroys homes. It is usually pretty easy to tell if a person is a drunk. His breath stinks, his eyes are red, he is perpetually dumb from all of the brain cells he has killed, and he can't pay the bills because he spends the money on booze. But a person who is into pornography can often go for years undetected, come to church all the time, seem so respectable, keep it all hidden until it blows up and the home is destroyed in a public spectacle.

The statistics on pornography are truly frightening. If they are true, then it is possible that I am preaching this very moment to some folks who partake of pornography. You can feel the blood flushing to your face, because you know it's you, and you hope no one else knows it's you. Listen to me well: if you don't get that influence out of your life forever, you will eventually lose everything you really love; wife, kids, home, friends, reputation. Porn will take it all.

Look at how serious Job took this: **Job 31:1** *I made a covenant with mine eyes; why then should I think upon a maid?*

Look at how serious Jesus took this: **Matthew 5:28** *But I say unto you, That whosoever looketh on a woman to lust after her hath committed adultery with her already in his heart.*

118

We need to take it just as serious.

So how can we guard against it?

Never start.

No one ever got addicted to anything without doing it the first time. You will be tempted to pick up that first magazine, or watch that first video. But in today's world, you will probably first be tempted to click that mouse. I'll say more about that in a moment, but just know for now that the best way you can preserve your home from the destruction that pornography brings is to never start.

Never put yourself in any position where you could be influenced by it.

Romans 13:14 *But put ye on the Lord Jesus Christ, and make not provision for the flesh, to fulfil the lusts thereof.*

There are certain stores I will not go into because of the magazines that I know will be there. There are certain people I will not hang around because I know they might expose me to it.

Never ever hang around somebody who likes smut!

Girls, never ever date or marry some guy who looks at pornography. Trust a pastor who has counseled a lot of people: if you marry a guy who looks at pornography, you are marrying an eventual hell on earth.

You may be thinking, "How will I know? It's not like he's going to tell me!"

Maybe not. But do you know what I have found to be true? Usually, he will tell someone, and that information will normally find it's way to the girl. What normally happens, though, is that your parents or your friends or your pastor are the ones that find out, and they try to warn the girl, but the guy denies it, and the girl believes him. Before you label everyone but your guy a liar, you might want to back up, extend the time period, and do some investigating.

Be "online accountable."

My best defense against ever falling for this is the fact that my wife knows more about computers than I do. I intentionally keep it that way! I will never try to learn more than her, because I know that as long as she knows more than I do, I won't even be tempted to do something stupid.

Whatever it takes, you need to ensure that pornography never becomes a part of your life or your home. If it already has, whether you are a man, woman, boy or girl, you need to get right with God, because He is the main one you are hurting by what you are doing. The Christ who hung on Calvary for you despises pornography. It makes a mockery of the gift of sexuality that He gave to be enjoyed only between a husband and a wife. Pornography brings a stranger into your relationship, a stranger that will ruin you relationship with God and with your spouse.

Booze.

Proverbs 20:1 *Wine is a mocker, strong drink is raging: and whosoever is deceived thereby is not wise.*

One of the most socially acceptable sins of our times is drinking. Yet it is one of the most consistent destroyers of homes.

When we first started the church, I got to try and help a guy named Bob. Bob had tons of potential. He was an excellent musician, and had a lot of job skills. But Bob had lost it all. He had a couple of little kids that he wasn't even allowed to be near. He had a wife and an ex-wife that he wasn't allowed to be near. He had no license. He couldn't hold down a job. He had pawned his guitar. I mean this guy had literally lost it all.

How? Obvious answer, booze. He couldn't stay away from the bottle. I remember driving down the road with him in the side seat of my car, talking to him. He was always mullygrubbing about how bad he had it. He said to me "If I had a good woman like you do, I could do right too!" I said, "You've got it backwards, Bob. If you did right, you could have a good woman like I've got!"

Booze makes you an idiot. I was at home on a Saturday night. 2:00 a.m. came, and my phone rang. It was Bob on the other line. He said, "Preacher, if I commit suicide, will I go to hell?" I talked to him till he finally fell asleep. Next Saturday night, 2:00 a.m., ring ring,

"Preacher, if I commit suicide, will I go to hell?" I talked to him till he finally fell asleep again, but I was hot. I told my wife "If he calls again next Saturday at 2:00 a.m., I'm gonna tell him, 'You'll fry like a tater tot in the hottest part of hell if you commit suicide!'" It may not have been true, but I was mad enough to say it anyway. Well the call didn't come in at 2:00 a.m. the next Saturday night. It was 4:00 a.m. This time the voice said, "I did it. Goodbye, Preacher. Click." I tried calling back, no answer. I dialed 911, told them the situation, got out of bed, got dressed, got in my car and drove 45 minutes to his house. The ambulance was there when I got there. The paramedic said, "Preacher, you need to talk to him. He took a bunch of sleeping pills. It's not a lethal dose, but combined with the booze it is dangerous and he does need to go to the hospital, but he's refusing to go."

I went over to him and said, "Bob, listen to me very carefully. If you don't get into that ambulance, it's going to be fatal, because I'm about five seconds from killing you myself!" He got in the ambulance, and off we went to the hospital. I sat there just outside his room in the ER. His mom had shown up, she was sitting beside me. Her drunk-of-a-son was in the room, giving the nurses who were trying to get him to use the little hand-held bathroom a miserable time. Finally, one of them came storming out, and I heard her say, "Looks like we get to do this the hard way..." A moment later, a Godzilla sized nurse came crashing down the hallway. She was carrying a catheter... and wearing an evil grin that said, "I love my job."

She went into that room, and a minute later I heard a drunken, slurred voice say "I told you I'm not gonna WHOA! I'LL PEE, I'LL PEE, I'LL PEE, I'LL PEE, I'LL PEE!" Too late!

And while I was sitting outside that room, beside his mom, desperately trying not to laugh, something inside of me was saying, "This is what booze will bring a person to, son."

What woman wants to live with a person like that?

If you are single and drink, you will not be able to get a good girl to marry you, because they have better sense. If you are married and start drinking, you will probably lose your wife and your kids if you have them, because no woman wants to put up with a man who drinks away the bill money, gets violently angry, stays out all night, and stinks like booze.

I hear people all the time say, "Well they drank wine in the Bible!" People that say that have never done an ounce of homework. There is not one bit of resemblance between what the Bible calls wine and any alcoholic beverage produced today.

Today, alcoholic beverages have alcohol added by both natural and artificial processes. First of all, in Bible times, both non-fermented and fermented grape juice was called wine. So any time you see it positively spoken of, you know it is talking about non-fermented grape juice. We know that because **Proverbs 23:31** says: *Look not thou upon the wine when it is red, when it giveth his colour in the cup, when it moveth itself aright.*

That is a description of fermented wine, and the Bible says "don't even look at it, much less drink it!"

But here is where things get even more interesting. In Bible days, fermentation was done by natural processes; alcohol was not added by artificial means like it is today. That process led to no more that 2% alcohol content. But then, it was watered down 4 parts water to 1 part wine. Do the math and you come up with less than one half of one percent alcohol content! So don't ever try to tell me "I can drink because the Bible talks about wine!" You better do your homework and get a lot smarter than that.

Alcohol will destroy a home. I spent years ministering down at the homeless shelter. Pretty much everyone there has a busted home, and 99% of them lost their homes and families due to booze.

I have been to many rescue missions, and the same statistics hold true.

My stepfather was bad when he was sober; he was an unholy terror when drinking.

Young people, guy or girl, especially those of you in public schools, you are going to be tempted to drink. If you love God, you won't. If you want to one day have a decent marriage, you won't. If you want to end up a loser, you will. If you want to live in a run-down shack for life, you will.

You need to choose now. You need to choose to be an absolute teetotaler, never coming near booze.

Here is the security system you need to have in place to make sure your home is not destroyed by this vile enemy.

Never start drinking. Never take the first sip. You need to decide now that you are going to go an entire lifetime without ever having the first drop of alcohol cross your lips.

Never ever get around people that drink. **Proverbs 23:20** *Be not among winebibbers* **(people who drink)***; among riotous eaters of flesh* **(people who party)***:*

Did you get that? It's in your Bible. You're not to be around people who drink. You're not to be around people who party.

Hey, Young People, that rules out grad week or spring break all together.

When I was a senior, I decided I was going to go to the beach on spring break. My mother had a cow. She said "O, no you're not!" I said "O, Yes I am!" She said "O, no you're not!" I said "O, Yes I am!" She said "O, no you're not!" I said "O, Yes I am!"

Guess what? O, No I didn't! And I thank God for it a thousand times over.

Hey, Adults, this "never get around people that drink" thing applies to you as well.

Sometimes, I just hate being right, but I'm usually right whether I hate it or not. Something about thinking Biblically that causes that. A few years ago, I talked to a man who had made a profession of faith, and gotten out of booze, and gotten his marriage back together right. Well, he got into a financial bind. His solution was to move back near his mom, dad, brother sister etc, so that he could live in a home on their property and not have to pay rent. The problem was, it was his family that got him drinking to begin with. I told him "Sir, you cannot move back there. If you do, I promise you, you will end up drinking again, and it will be worse than before." He said, "Preacher I don't have a choice, I can't afford to live anywhere else." I said, "Sir, you can't afford to live there. It will cost you your home. If you have to pitch a giant tent in my back yard, so be it, but do not move back there."

He ignored my counsel. He was drinking again within three months, worse than ever. His booze has cost him everything, and it was not necessary. All he had to do was follow one simple piece of advice, "do not be among wine-bibbers." I don't care if they are friends, or mama, or daddy, or brother or sister, don't get around people who drink. Let them sober up, and invite them to come to where you are, no alcohol allowed.

By the way, another word to the young people who are thinking of getting married one day: If he or she drinks, even a little bit, mark them off your list right now. It's one of the best things you will ever do for your future marriage.

I have taken my own advice. I once dated a gorgeous girl, and then found out she likes to drink. That relationship was over, right then and there. And look what God gave me instead!

Let's deal with the third home killer that you need to secure against.

Infidelity

Hebrews 13:4 *Marriage is honourable in all, and the bed undefiled: but whoremongers and adulterers God will judge.*

Look at another passage on this subject: **Proverbs 6:27** *Can a man take fire in his bosom, and his clothes not be burned? 28 Can one go upon hot coals, and his feet not be burned? 29 So he that goeth in to his neighbour's wife; whosoever toucheth her shall not be innocent. 30 Men do not despise a thief, if he steal to satisfy his soul when he is hungry; 31 But if he be found, he shall restore sevenfold; he shall give all the substance of his house. 32 But whoso committeth adultery with a woman lacketh understanding: he that doeth it destroyeth his own soul. 33 A wound and dishonour shall he get; and his reproach shall not be wiped away. 34 For jealousy is the rage of a man: therefore he* *will not spare in the day of vengeance. 35 He will not regard any ransom; neither will he rest content, though thou givest many gifts.*

There is nothing in the world so destructive as an affair, infidelity, or, as the Bible puts it, *adultery.*

This sin is a destroyer of homes that seem so strong you are shocked beyond measure when you hear of it:

The former vice-president of a worldwide family radio ministry spoke often on the subject of marriage. But then one day, his familiar voice that always opened up the broadcast wasn't there anymore. He had been caught in an affair. A man who spoke to millions every day about not committing adultery, committed adultery.

Thirty-five minutes from here, there is a church that was pastored by a man from right here in Cleveland County, a man about my age. Solid man, solid home. He was removed from the church a few years ago for adultery; he has lost his family and his ministry.

Let me ask you all this: how many of you knew a marriage that you thought would last forever, but then were shocked to find out that there had been adultery, and the marriage was dead?

There is no violation of trust so great as this one.

Now let me say up front what is normally saved for last on this subject. An affair does not have to destroy a home. If it is confessed and forsaken, you can forgive him or her like Christ forgave you on Calvary. And if you do, you will earn more love from that forgiven spouse than you could ever imagine.

But let's see if we can't keep that from happening in the first place. What kind of security system can we put in place against it?

First of all, we can keep our virginity till marriage.

2 Timothy 2:22 *Flee also youthful lusts: but follow righteousness, faith, charity, peace, with them that call on the Lord out of a pure heart.*

You may say "Now wait a minute preacher, I know that's important, but what in the world does it have to do with keeping my future marriage from going through adultery?"

Here's what. A lot of adultery is caused by comparison. More people than you can imagine have had sex before marriage, and then they get married, and their spouse does not compare in their mind to what they have already had. So they eventually go out looking. Being a virgin till marriage will fix that.

You know what? As far as I know, my wife is the world's greatest lover. But truth be told, she may be awful. I have no way of knowing, I have no-one to compare her to.

As far as my wife knows, I'm a regular Don Juan. But for all we both know, I could be Goober from Mayberry.

Hey, we're both as happy as we can be (right, Honey? Honey?)

As a bonus, I never have to worry about someone coming to my wife and telling her "He may not have told you, but I slept with him before you did." If anybody ever tried that, my wife would laugh herself silly. See, she was there on our honeymoon. Man, I needed cue cards and cliff notes and a map to figure things out!

Because we were both virgins, neither of us feels any pressure of comparison, so we aren't out looking!

Second, we can remember that a vow is a vow.

Ecclesiastes 5:4 *When thou vowest a vow unto God, defer not to pay it; for he hath no pleasure in fools: pay that which thou hast vowed. 5 Better is it that thou shouldest not vow, than that thou shouldest vow and not pay.*

I think married couples take this "vow thing" way too lightly. Before you go off and have an affair, you need to re-read that vow you made, especially that "for better or for worse" part!

Third, we can refuse to ever put ourselves in a position where we even have the opportunity to do wrong.

Romans 13:14 *But put ye on the Lord Jesus Christ, and **make not provision for the flesh, to fulfil the lusts thereof.***

Don't even give yourself an opportunity. Do you realize that as much as I dislike her, I have never spit on Rosie O'Donnell? Why is that? Among other reasons, I have never been near her; I have never had the opportunity.

If you never have the opportunity to be unfaithful, you will never be unfaithful.

I see preachers so often that go and preach revivals alone, leaving their family at home. That to me is begging for trouble. If I can't take my wife, or my wife's family, I'm not going.

Some of you new folks may think it odd to see a pastor whose wife is also his secretary. There are some really good reasons for it. First of all, she is a really good secretary. But more importantly, I figure if I, as a pastor, am going to be tempted to chase my secretary around the desk, I may as well be able to catch her!

How often do any of you see me when Miss Dana is not either with me, or somewhere nearby? Not very often! If I am ever going to cheat on my wife, I'm going to have to get her permission!

Men, ladies, however you need to do it, find a way to make sure that you are cut off from even having the chance to cheat. Don't be alone in a place where you could have someone else come to you. Never ever, ever, ever go on "business dates" with a member of the opposite sex. Never develop inappropriate "friendships" with a member of the opposite sex.

In 14 years of marriage, I have never allowed myself an opportunity to cheat, and because of that, I've never cheated.

It was when David the king gave himself the opportunity that he fell.

Fourth, we can make sure that spouses keep spouses satisfied.

I've already devoted an entire chapter to this, so I'm not going to say much here, but I do want to give you a pertinent passage of Scripture to consider: **1 Corinthians 7:3** *Let the husband render unto the wife due benevolence: and likewise also the wife unto the husband. 4 The wife hath not power of her own body, but the husband: and likewise also the husband hath not power of his own body, but the* *wife. 5 Defraud ye not one the other, except it be with consent for a time, that ye may give yourselves to fasting and prayer; and come together again, that Satan tempt you not for your incontinency.*

Dissatisfaction at home leads to the devil having a chance to tempt people to infidelity.

Last, we can make a list of the cost, and burn it into our minds and hearts forever.

Here are a few of the consequences that the Bible mentions to adultery:

Broken fellowship with God - Psalm 51 (written by David after his adultery with Bathsheba)

Broken relationship with man. Bathsheba lost her husband due to this adultery.

Incurring the wrath of man - Proverbs 6:27-35

Possible venereal disease - Psalm 38:1-7 (also written by David after his adultery with Bathsheba)

A guilty conscience - Psalm 51:3 "My sin is ever before me!"

The judging hand of God - Hebrews 13:4

Church discipline upon the non-repentant - I Corinthians 5:9-13

Do you realize that all of these home-destroying sins are sins of our own making? They are sins that people *choose* to engage in:

Thomas Costain's history, <u>The Three Edwards</u>, described the life of Raynald III, a fourteenth-century duke in what is now Belgium. Raynald was extremely obese. So much so that he was given a Latin nickname, Crassus, which means "fat."

After a violent quarrel, Raynald's younger brother Edward led a successful revolt against him. Edward captured Raynald but did not kill him. Instead, he built a room around Raynald in the Nieuwkerk castle and promised him he could regain his title and property as soon as he was able to leave the room.

This would not have been difficult for most people since the room had several windows and a door of near-normal size, and none was locked or barred. The problem was Raynald's size. To regain his freedom, he needed to lose weight. But Edward knew his older brother, and each day he sent a variety of delicious foods and sweets into that room. Instead of ignoring the sweets and dieting his way out of prison, Raynald grew bigger by the day.

A person who found out about this went to Duke Edward and accused him of cruelty. But Edward answered: "My brother is not a prisoner. He may leave when he so wills."

Raynald was caught in a trap that he could have gotten out of any time he liked. All he had to do was give up that which was ruining him. Just like a lot of people who are right now being voluntarily ruined by pornography, booze, and unfaithfulness.

PART ELEVEN:
WINDOWS, WONDERFUL WINDOWS

Y ou probably heard about the newlyweds. On their honeymoon, the groom took his bride by the hand and said, "Now that we're married, dear, I hope you won't mind if I mention a few little defects that I've noticed about you."

"Not at all," the bride replied with a deceptive sweetness. "It was those little defects that kept me from getting a better husband."

After we got the new church building all enclosed with metal roof and metal walls, the feeling of it really changed, and I mean for the worse. We had lights hanging up, we had fans running, but it really didn't help much. We would be in that building working, sweating, baking, and the entire atmosphere of the building would just be dark, oppressive, and heavy. But then, we'd make our way through the building, and open up every one of the fourteen windows, and an amazing transformation would take place. A nice breeze would start to blow through, and within a few minutes the air felt less heavy, it wasn't as dark, everything just felt a lot better.

That reminds me so much of something I often see in homes. There is a monster that kills so many homes and relationships. It turns everything dark, heavy, and oppressive. And most people just don't know how to open the windows and let a fresh breeze from heaven blow through and change things. That monster that I am talking about is depression.

When depression gets into a home, nothing good ever comes of it. When a spouse gets depressed, (not sad; sad is a different matter. Sad will go away, sad can be handled) intimacy stops being what it should, or ceases altogether. When a spouse gets depressed, those happy mealtimes talking together will stop. When a spouse gets depressed, every molehill becomes a mountain. When a spouse gets depressed, the other spouse will feel more alone than if they actually were alone.

When a child gets depressed it isn't much better. A child getting depressed will put a heavy strain on a man and wife's relationship, because so much of their time and attention will be on that child. It will even affect any other children in the home, because they will feel the affects of mom and dad not giving them much attention, since all of it is going to the depressed child.

Clearly, depression needs to be dealt with and defeated in the home. I want to do my best to teach you how to open the windows, let the fresh breezes blow, and make sure that it never ever has a chance to ruin your home.

One of the world's finest preachers lived from 1834-1892. But what most people do not know is that frequently during his ministry he was plunged into severe depression, due in part to gout but also for other reasons. In a biography of this preacher, Arnold Dallimore wrote, "What he suffered in those times of darkness we may not know; even his desperate calling on God brought no relief. 'There are dungeons', this preacher said, 'beneath the castles of despair.'" This depressed preacher was none other than the great C.H. Spurgeon.[2]

Many years ago a young midwestern lawyer suffered from such deep depression that his friends thought it best to keep all knives and razors out of his reach. He questioned his life's calling and the prudence of even attempting to follow it through. During this time he wrote, "I am now the most miserable man living. Whether I shall ever be better, I cannot tell. I awfully forebode I shall not."

This depressed lawyer also had a name you might recognize, Abraham Lincoln.[3]

Depression is an all too common problem that homes face, sometimes in mom, sometimes in dad, sometimes even in the kids. People everywhere seem drawn to depression, and unaware of how to deal with it.

So what is this awful monster that so many people face? The Encyclopedia Britannica defines depression as:

"A neurotic or psychotic disorder marked by sadness, inactivity, difficulty in thinking and concentration, a significant increase or decrease in appetite and time spent sleeping, feelings of dejection and hopelessness, and sometimes suicidal tendencies."

Hippocrates, thousands of years ago, called it Melancholia. Researchers from the University of Texas call depression the "common cold of mental health." A somewhat bizarre website defines depression as "the denial of God."

You see, then, that there is no blanket one size fits all definition of depression. We are dealing with a problem that does not even have a common, universally accepted identity. Fortunately, we have the Bible. And though the Bible does not use the word depression, it clearly shows us an example of someone who any counselor, secular or Christian, would have to classify as depressed! So looking at this example, we can learn a bit about God's definition of depression, and how to defeat it.

1 Kings 19:1 *And Ahab told Jezebel all that Elijah had done, and withal how he had slain all the prophets with the sword. 2 Then Jezebel sent a messenger unto Elijah, saying, So let the gods do to me, and more also, if I make not thy life as the life of one of them by to morrow about this time. 3 And when he saw that, he arose, and went for his life, and came to Beersheba, which belongeth to Judah, and left his servant there. 4 But he himself went a day's journey into the wilderness, and came and sat down under a juniper tree: and he requested for himself that he might die; and said, It is enough; now, O LORD, take away my life; for I am not better than my fathers.*

Amazingly, the clearest example of a person battling depression is none other than the great prophet Elijah. It is evident from this episode in his life that depression can be Biblically defined this way:

A period of extreme hopelessness, characterized by erratic behavior and irrational thought.

Elijah was not just worried; he was hopeless. He did not see any light at the end of the tunnel. He also ran from a fight, which was completely out of character for him. He had just won a victory against 850 false prophets, and called down fire from God out of heaven! Yet he then turns and runs from a woman. That is why we say that depression is characterized by irrational behavior. Any man that whips 850 other men and then runs from a woman jolly well better be depressed, because that is irrational behavior. Someone may stop sleeping, or sleep all the time. They may quit a job, or work 120 hours a week non-stop. They may withdraw from friends, family, or society in general. It can be anything, but a person who is depressed will normally exhibit some erratic behavior, if you are perceptive enough to see it.

Elijah then demonstrated irrational thought. He ran for his life, and then begged to die. If he really wanted to die, all he had to do was go back! Elijah was absolutely depressed. But the good news is that he overcame that depression, and God gave us a record of it. Somehow, he was able to open the windows and let the fresh breezes blow into his soul one more time.

First, when battling depression, deal as much as possible with the physical and behavioral causes that make the body not operate the way that God designed it.

When a secular counselor deals with a person that is depressed, the term "chemical imbalance" will almost invariably arise. That is why most secular counselors end up treating depression with medication. Prescription drugs are hooking people by the millions into a life-long dependency. The war on drugs rails against crack cocaine, marijuana, LSD, and methamphetamines, but gives a pass to things that in many cases are just as addictive. The difference is that a doctor, rather than a dealer, is the recipient of the profits.

And it is at this juncture that many fundamental Christian counselors make a mistake. We hear the term "chemical imbalance" thrown about so consistently, and we shout to the hilltops that there is no such thing as a chemical imbalance. I disagree. The human body, designed by God, is loaded with chemicals. The human brain, designed by God, is loaded with chemicals. It is just as possible for something to go wrong with the chemicals within your body as it is for something to go wrong with your heart, or lungs, or kidneys. So I do not agree with people who say that there is no such thing as a chemical imbalance. But I also do not agree with people who consistently dope people up to fix that chemical imbalance. Both are wrong, both ignore how God designed our body and mind.

I am also not saying that there is never a time for medication. I am saying point blank, though, that medication, which should be a very last resort, is almost always used as the first resort instead. I am saying that many doctors and psychiatrists try to treat spiritual and behavioral problems with drugs, rather than actually get to the heart of the matter. I am saying we live in the medication generation, and that the vast majority of people who are doped up on anti-depressants and anxiety medication probably have better options available to them.

When someone comes to you battling depression, you can help them deal with any chemical imbalance they may have, by dealing with the physical and behavioral causes that keep their body chemicals out of whack. Let's look at some things from this episode in the life of Elijah:

We observe first of all that when Elijah was battling depression, he got some rest.

1 Kings 19:5 *And as he lay and slept under a juniper tree, behold, then an angel touched him, and said unto him, Arise and eat.* **6** *And he looked, and, behold, there was a cake baken on the coals, and* *a cruse of water at his head. And he did eat and drink, and laid him down again.*

Twice, Elijah slept. This idea of restoring a proper amount of sleep and rest is essential in dealing with depression. Elijah was exhausted. He had run for his life, he was in the wilderness. He was too tired *not* to be depressed.

It is amazing how intricately God designed the human body. For years, people have been sleeping and resting, and not even really knowing all the good it does. The human body is literally a chemical producing factory, and the time that it does its best work is when the body is getting rest and sleep. Your body produces scores of helpful chemicals, both in the body and the brain, when your body is at rest. If you want to treat a chemical imbalance, this is an excellent place to start. God knew this, and He told us so over and over:

Genesis 2:2 *And on the seventh day God ended his work which he had made; and he rested on the seventh day from all his work which he had made. 3 And God blessed the seventh day, and sanctified it: because that in it he had rested from all his work which God created and made.*

God Himself, who did not need rest, took some anyway to set an example that we are to rest! He even set aside a day for it. Look at more:

Exodus 16:30 *So the people rested on the seventh day.*

Exodus 23:12 *Six days thou shalt do thy work, and on the seventh day thou shalt rest: that thine ox and thine ass may rest, and the son of thy handmaid, and the stranger, may be refreshed.*

Mark 6:31 *And he said unto them, Come ye yourselves apart into a desert place, and rest a while: for there were many coming and going, and they had no leisure so much as to eat.*

It is no wonder America is the most depressed country on earth; we consistently violate God's command that we give our body rest. In so doing, we either get depressed, or run our families into depression, like the preacher in a Northern state who liked to say

"there's no rest for the wicked, and the righteous don't need any."
Until his wife had a nervous breakdown.

A second thing to notice is that when Elijah was battling
depression, he got some good nourishment.

1 Kings 19:5 *And as he lay and slept under a juniper tree,
behold, then an angel touched him, and said unto him, Arise and eat.* **6**
*And he looked, and, behold, there was a cake baken on the coals, and
a cruse of water at his head. And he did eat and drink, and laid him
down again.* **7** *And the angel of the LORD came again the second time,
and touched him, and said, Arise and eat; because the journey is too
great for thee.*

Twice, Elijah was fed a good meal. No preservatives, no junk
food, nothing unhealthy. Our body takes the nourishment we give it,
and converts it to the chemicals and energy that we need to function.
It is no wonder people are often depressed. A livermush and grease
biscuit for breakfast, a Big Mac combo for lunch, and a bag of potato
chips and a soda for supper, week after week after week. Talk about a
chemical imbalance! Eating poorly wrecks your physical condition
and depression is a logical result. Many times when we are helping
members through a depression, we take them out and treat them to a
meal. This is not just to get them to come out into the sunshine again,
it is also so that we can get them somewhere that has actual green
vegetables, lean meats, and other good things to eat. Feed your
automobile grease burgers from Hardee's for a year or two and see if it
doesn't get depressed!

The third thing we see is that when Elijah was battling
depression, he got some good exercise

1 Kings 19:8 *And he arose, and did eat and drink, and went in
the strength of that meat forty days and forty nights unto Horeb the
mount of God.*

Please consider this. How many of you feel like you are a bit out of shape, you get winded pretty easily, and you wish you felt better than you do?

Second question: how good of a shape do you think you could be in if you went on a forty day walk?

Third question: how good do you think you would feel after you stepped on the scale, or looked in the mirror, after that forty day walk? Not feeling so depressed anymore, are we?

But there is much more to this thing of exercise than just what we read on the scale or see in the mirror. Remember that thing of chemical imbalance that we spoke of? Exercising does a marvelous thing in regards to that. When a person exercises, their body does exactly what it was designed by God to do. It produces a wonderful set of chemicals known as endorphins. There are three basic kinds that our body produces during exercise. Beta endorphins, enkaphalins, and dynorphin. These marvelous chemicals, when produced by the body, reduce pain, produce feelings of happiness and euphoria, help to regulate the appetite, and settle the mind. There are very few things on earth that are as powerful as endorphins at fixing a faulty body chemistry, and making depression vanish like the night when the sun rises. Incidentally, these are also the exact same chemicals and chemical reactions that every anti-depressant drug on earth seeks to mimic! So which is more likely to be better; the natural, or that which tries to mimic the natural? Always try the natural first. When someone comes into my office huffing and puffing and wheezing from the strenuous walk of fifty feet that it took them to get there, it doesn't surprise me a bit that they are depressed. The scale depresses them, the mirror depresses them, the size clothes they are wearing depresses them, and the fact that their body has less endorphins than a liberal has good ideas depresses them.

So when dealing with depression, deal as much as possible with the physical and behavioral causes that make the body not operate the way that God designed it.

When dealing with depression, deal also with the spiritual, emotional, and relational causes that contribute to depression.

When Elijah was battling depression, he came to where God was.

1 Kings 19:8 *And he arose, and did eat and drink, and went in the strength of that meat forty days and forty nights unto Horeb the mount of God.*

Horeb was where Moses met God in the burning bush. Horeb was where God gave millions of Jews water from the rock. Horeb is where God made a covenant with Israel. Elijah knew that he could meet with God in Horeb.

When a person that is depressed runs the opposite way from where they can meet with God, they will stay depressed and it will get worse. When a person who is depressed runs toward God as hard as they can, the exact opposite will be true.

This is why lost people have to be medicated. They have never met God, they do not know Him, He does not dwell in their heart. The lost person does not have what God can give to fix depression, the pardon from sin, the peace that passes all understanding, and the power for daily living. But a Christian can become just as weak and depressed as a lost person when they stray from a close walk with God.

There is a dear lady in our church that we worked with concerning her depression some years back. Invariably, she made the same mistake over and over again. The happier she was, the more likely she was to be faithful to God's house. But whenever she felt herself slipping into a depression, she withdrew, and missed several services in a row. I remember a time in particular that God gave me a message through my devotions that I knew would be of infinite help to her. As I put it on paper, God let me see her face, and her situation. If I have even known a message that was given by God to help someone, this was it. She showed up that morning, walked in the door... and then a second later turned around and walked back out. She told me later that she was just too depressed to stay. She allowed her depression to keep her from a God-given message to help fix it.

Never slack in your prayer, Bible reading, and personal devotions during times of depression. Grasp after them as a drowning man does to a lifeline, for they are your salvation during those deadly times! Never miss a service, never miss an opportunity to be with the saints of God, never miss a chance to hear the songs of Zion, never miss a chance to get to the altar. When you are battling depression, get to where God is meeting with His people!

When Elijah was battling depression, God also corrected his wrong perception of reality.

Elijah said: **1 Kings 19:14** *And he said, I have been very jealous for the LORD God of hosts: because the children of Israel have forsaken thy covenant, thrown down thine altars, and slain thy prophets with the sword; and **I, even I only, am left**; and they seek my life, to take it away.*

God said: **Kings 19:18** *Yet **I have left me seven thousand** in Israel, all the knees which have not bowed unto Baal, and every mouth which hath not kissed him.*

A person battling depression will very rarely have the right view of reality. If he is facing a molehill, he will make a mountain out of it. If he is facing a mountain, he will turn it into an entire mountain range. He will normally focus exclusively on the problems, and ignore the blessings altogether. A depressed person needs to do a good inventory, and see just how very blessed he is, and how very good God has been to him. A person living under a delusion will not get out of his depression. When someone comes to me battling depression, I normally get him to take a piece of paper, and write some words on it, words like: *Mom, dad, kids, brother, sister, house, car, sight, hearing, the ability to walk, sense of smell, freedom, the Bible, salvation, Heaven.*

What I am pointing out is how very blest most depressed people are! If you are battling depression, you need to do inventory.

Notice also that when Elijah was battling depression, God turned his focus away from himself, and his pity party, and made him go serve others.

1 Kings 19:15 *And the LORD said unto him, Go, return on thy way to the wilderness of Damascus: and when thou comest, anoint Hazael to be king over Syria: 16 And Jehu the son of Nimshi shalt thou anoint to be king over Israel: and Elisha the son of Shaphat of Abelmeholah shalt thou anoint to be prophet in thy room.*

There are very few things as powerful for curing depression as going out and serving others. It is hard to be pathetic when you are wheeling an old person into an activity room for a nursing home service. It is hard to be depressed when you are tending to the fatherless, and ministering to widows. The more a person focuses on self, the more prone he will be to get depressed. When a person is depressed, he needs to get engaged in serving others. That will give him one thing he truly needs in life, <u>a purpose</u>.

Everybody needs a reason to live, and every body can have one if they want it.

Let me tell you this point blank. If you are sitting around whining about how bad your childhood was, or how hard life has been on you, or how mean people have been to you, you will stay depressed.

If you are pouting and whining because someone has done you wrong, and you refuse to forgive them and move on, you will stay depressed

Here is my advice, and it will work: cancel the pity party. Put away the black streamers, and the kazoos that are all in a minor key. Turn your focus away from yourself, forgive every wrong ever done to you, get off of your hind end, and go out and serve others. There were two young ladies in my church, both of whom had experienced awful things in their lives. One had been abandoned, the other had experienced the death of a parent. These girls were the same age, and were alike in many regards. Both of them went into a severe depression. But today, one is still in that depression, and the other is as happy as any human I have ever seen. There is one, and only one significant difference that I have been able to observe in them. The young lady who is still depressed after all these years has chosen to spend her life focused on herself and her own misery. She is in a downward spiral into darkness, and will probably never get out. The young lady who has beaten depression and walked out into the bright sunshine of life once more has taken the opposite approach. She has chosen to give her life to serving others. Each day finds her serving a group of senior citizens, and in making their life better, she has made her own better. I am so unbelievably proud of that dear young lady; she has shown wisdom far beyond her years.

When Elijah was battling depression, God also showed him the future.

1 Kings 19:17 *And it shall come to pass, that him that escapeth the sword of Hazael shall Jehu slay: and him that escapeth from the sword of Jehu shall Elisha slay.*

There were some wicked, wicked people that needed to be judged, and God showed Elijah that it would happen. When a person comes to you battling depression, he has a dark cloud hanging over his future. Take your Bible, and show him what the future is like for the child of God!

1 Thessalonians 4:16 *For the Lord himself shall descend from heaven with a shout, with the voice of the archangel, and with the trump of God: and the dead in Christ shall rise first:* **17** *Then we which are alive and remain shall be caught up together with them in the clouds, to meet the Lord in the air: and so shall we ever be with the Lord.*

1 Corinthians 15:51 *Behold, I shew you a mystery; We shall not all sleep, but we shall all be changed,* **52** *In a moment, in the twinkling of an eye, at the last trump: for the trumpet shall sound, and the dead shall be raised incorruptible, and we shall be changed.* **53** *For this corruptible must put on incorruption, and this mortal must put on immortality.* **54** *So when this corruptible shall have put on* *incorruption, and this mortal shall have put on immortality, then shall be brought to pass the saying that is written, Death is swallowed up in victory.*

Revelation 19:11 *And I saw heaven opened, and behold a white horse; and he that sat upon him was called Faithful and True, and in righteousness he doth judge and make war. 12 His eyes were as a flame of fire, and on his head were many crowns; and he had a name written, that no man knew, but he himself. 13 And he was clothed with a vesture dipped in blood: and his name is called The Word of God. 14 And the armies which were in heaven followed him upon white horses, clothed in fine linen, white and clean. 15 And out of his mouth goeth a sharp sword, that with it he should smite the nations: and he shall rule them with a rod of iron: and he treadeth the winepress of the fierceness and wrath of Almighty God. 16 And he hath on his vesture and on his thigh a name written, KING OF KINGS, AND LORD OF LORDS.*

What a future! It is difficult to remain in a state of depression when our eyes are drinking in our future state of glory!

Finally, when Elijah was battling depression, God directed him to godly companionship.

1 Kings 19:16 *And Jehu the son of Nimshi shalt thou anoint to be king over Israel: and Elisha the son of Shaphat of Abelmeholah shalt thou anoint to be prophet in thy room.*

1 Kings 19:19 *So he departed thence, and found Elisha the son of Shaphat, who was plowing with twelve yoke of oxen before him, and he with the twelfth: and Elijah passed by him, and cast his mantle upon him. 20 And he left the oxen, and ran after Elijah, and said, Let me, I pray thee, kiss my father and my mother, and then I will follow thee. And he said unto him, Go back again: for what have I done to thee? 21 And he returned back from him, and took a yoke of oxen, and slew them, and boiled their flesh with the instruments of the oxen, and gave unto the people, and they did eat. Then he arose, and went after Elijah, and ministered unto him.*

From this point forward, Elijah and Elisha had godly companionship together. Loneliness is the ally of depression; companionship is the enemy of depression.

Understand this fully, though. This relationship was not one where Elijah was weak and simpering and whiny and expected Elisha to make him feel better all the time. Elisha did minister to Elijah, but the truth is that Elijah poured his life into Elisha. Elijah took Elisha from being a farm boy, and made a prophet out of him. In other words, Elijah, far from whining that he did not have any friends, went out and befriended someone.

I will never forget the time a lady visited our church, and my wife and I went to her home to visit her the next week. We found out quickly that she was as depressed as could be.

So I asked her, "Ma'am, when was the last time you went and paid someone a visit just to cheer them up?" She said, "Nobody ever comes to visit me to cheer me up." I said, "Um, when is the last time you ever picked up your phone and called someone, just to let them know you appreciate them?" She said, "No-one ever does that for me." I said, "Ma'am, we're talking, but it's obvious I'm not getting through here. Listen carefully; let me try one more time. When is the last time you ever made somebody a cake, and took it over to them for no reason at all?" She said, "No-one has ever fixed me a cake like that." I said, "Ma'am, I can't help you, good luck."

There are people everywhere that need friends, and it is fairly simple to make friends of them:

Proverbs 18:24 *A man that hath friends must shew himself friendly: and there is a friend that sticketh closer than a brother.*

You never again read of Elijah going into a depression, because he spent the rest of his life being a friend to someone.

In 1835 a man visited a doctor in Florence, Italy. He was filled with anxiety and exhausted from lack of sleep. He couldn't eat, and he avoided his friends. The doctor examined him and found that he was in prime physical condition. Concluding that his patient needed to have a good time, the physician told him about a circus in town and its star performer, a clown named Grimaldi. Night after night he had the people rolling in the aisles. "You must go and see him," the doctor advised. "Grimaldi is the world's funniest clown. He'll make you laugh and cure your sadness." "No," replied the despairing man, "he can't help me. You see, I am Grimaldi!"[4]

He was smiling on the outside, and dying on the inside. That is no way to live. It will not only wreck you, it may well wreck your home. It will be very hard on your spouse to stay with you and love you and enjoy your company if you are perpetually depressed. And you don't have to be like that. Why don't you open those wonderful windows and let the fresh breezes from heaven blow in.

PART TWELVE:
FRAMED FOR SUCCESS OR FRAMED FOR FAILURE

A man and his golfing buddy were on the seventh hole, getting ready to tee-off. At that moment, a funeral procession came down the road near to where they were. Bob backed away from the tee box, stood up straight, took off his cap, placed it over his heart, and bowed his head till the procession got all the way by.

His buddy was amazed. He said "Bob! I didn't know you had it in you! That was the most respectful thing I've ever seen."

Bob said, "Thanks, I appreciate that. Today would have been our 35th anniversary..."

Do you realize that we basically built a gymnasium on the new property? When we got that building enclosed, it was 10,400 feet of wide-open space. There were times we would be taking a break, and throwing a football back and forth to each other inside.

But today, in that same building, we don't have a gym anymore. What is the difference? We came in after the building was enclosed, and laid out metal track on the floor, in a specific pattern. Then we put corresponding metal track overhead in places, and started putting in metal studs. What we did was called "framing." We built walls and doors in that wide-open space. There isn't as much wide-open space anymore, but the building is much better because of it. If we had left it as is, imagine the confusing mess trying to have several Sunday school classes going at once. And how awkward would going to the bathroom have been? When we started laying out the framing, we came to a couple of spots where we had to change where the wall was going to go a bit, or alter an angle. We were avoiding pipes, or making sure that one room lined up with the next. We were intent on "framing for success."

There were a couple of plumbing problems I have told you about under the slab. Some we ripped up and changed, but in one case, I changed the wall in my bathroom to make sure that there wasn't going to be a pipe sticking up in the floor. It's just not good to have pipes sticking up in the middle of a room for no good reason!

When we got some of the lower walls done, we went in and attached a stud from the top of the wall to the purlins overhead, to keep the wall steady from now on. Again, we wanted the framing to be right. The framing sets the structure for the entire building. It determines how things work. If the framing isn't right, the building is in trouble.

Oh how well that applies in the home! There is a right way and a wrong way to frame a home. A home can be framed for success, or it can be framed for failure. And judging from what can be seen in the average American home these days, I think it is safe to say that a great many are framed for failure.

That isn't necessary. The reason we were able to frame our building for success is because we had a good set of blueprints to follow. And in your home, there is not just a good, but a *perfect* set of blueprints to follow, given to us by the very Creator and Architect of the home! So let's go over some of the blueprint, and see if we can get all of our homes to be framed for success.

We'll look at each point from the negative aspect, and then learn how to go from negative to positive. (And men, we are starting with you.)

When there is an authority figure in the home, without God being in charge, a home is framed for failure.

Colossians 1:16 *For by him were all things created, that are in heaven, and that are in earth, visible and invisible, whether they be thrones, or dominions, or principalities, or powers: all things were created by him, and for him: 17 And he is before all things, and by him all things consist. 18 And he is the head of the body, the church: who is the beginning, the firstborn from the dead; that in all things he might have the preeminence.*

This is where we deal with men who are in charge, without God being in charge.

This is how you end up with wicked, dead-beat men who expect their wives to obey no matter what. Newsflash buddy, you don't have that kind of authority! I listened to a radio broadcast a few years back, where a lady "teacher" was reading and answering letters. One was from a lady who said "Dear so and so. My husband is into pornography, and he wants me to come with him to a porno booth downtown, and go in and watch the porn flick with him. What should I do?" To which the teacherette responded "Oh dear one, just obey your husband. Maybe God will make him fall asleep so that you can close your eyes too and not have to actually watch it." God have mercy! I seem to recall much better advice from the apostle Peter who said "we ought to obey God rather than men!" (Acts 5:29) If you ask your wife to flagrantly disobey God, she has an obligation to disobey you! If I went to my wife and said "Honey, I want you to renounce Christ and become a Muslim," she wouldn't say "Yes dear, I will obey my husband no matter what," she would say, "No dear, I love you, but God comes first!" If I told her to murder one of our children, she would obey God by disobeying me. No human has a universal right to be obeyed in all circumstances.

We had a dear lady in our church whose husband demanded that she go out drinking with him. What was she to do? She did the only thing she could do in that circumstance, she obeyed God, and did not go. Was she being rebellious? No. Had he demanded that she go

149

on visitation with him, or that she clean the house, or that she do anything at all that did not violate Scripture, she would have done it gladly.

Men, you must understand that in order for you to truly be the head of your home, Christ must be the head of you. A godly wife will not have any problem obeying and submitting to a godly husband, because in so doing, she is submitting to God.

When there is a man who does not both lead and love, a home is framed for failure.

Ephesians 5:23 *For the husband is the head of the wife, even as Christ is the head of the church: and he is the saviour of the body.*

Ephesians 5:25 *Husbands, love your wives, even as Christ also loved the church, and gave himself for it;*

There is a word for a man who leads but does not love. That word is "tyrant." Castro leads, but he does not love. Hitler led, but he did not love. If you are intent on leading your wife without really loving her, you fit in the list along with them!

Joseph Stalin was not just a brutal dictator, he was also a lousy family man. He led both the nation and his home with an iron fist, but there was no love at all. His oldest son was named Yakov, and he was not a strong person. While still relatively young, he attempted suicide, and failed. Stalin detested his son, regarding him as weak and worthless. In 1941, Yakov was called up to war against Germany, and was eventually captured. Realizing whom they had taken, the Germans offered to exchange Yakov for a high-ranking Nazi prisoner of war. Stalin sent back a reply refusing their request, and calling his own son a traitor.

Stalin did not do any better with his other son Vasily, who became a drunk, or with his daughter Svetlana, who fled the country for India at the first opportunity. Stalin fancied that he had the ability to lead, but there is no real leadership that is not intertwined with love.

When there is a wife struggling for the reigns of power in the home, a home is framed for failure.

Ephesians 5:22 *Wives, submit yourselves unto your own husbands, as unto the Lord.*

I suspect this is among the least popular verses of Scripture in our modern day of feminism. But it is every much as Scriptural and binding as the command that we not steal, kill, or commit adultery. Every home must have a leader, and God is looking to the man as that leader. But, dear sir, may I point out what so many men seem to have missed? If you will *love* your wife like you should, she will likely have no problem letting you *lead* her! Submission is voluntary. You cannot "take it," your wife must "give it."

Ma'am, you should give it. By submitting to a godly husband, you are submitting to the Lord. It does not make you inferior in the least. My wife Dana is a <u>strong</u> lady in every way. She is smart, talented, and capable. Yet she allows me to lead, she allows me to be the head of the home, because she knows it is right. And in turn, I value her highly! I make her an equal part of every decision; I do nothing without her.

When either husband or wife undermines the other to the children, a home is framed for failure.

Exodus 20:12 *Honour thy father and thy mother: that thy days may be long upon the land which the LORD thy God giveth thee.*

I point to this verse in this place for one simple reason: a child is not likely to honor a parent if one of the parents dishonors the other! Some years ago we dealt with a home where the children were, in the parents words, "completely out of control." Mom and dad lamented the fact that the children "had no respect for them." Upon some inquiry, we soon found the root of the problem. One example should sum it up well: On one particular morning, the father got up early and fixed breakfast for the kids. Nothing elaborate, just peanut butter and jelly sandwiches (otherwise known as PBJ's). The mother heard the kids begin to literally scream at the father, because *he had not cut the crust off of the bread.* Now what does a smart mother do at this point? A smart mother applies the "rod of correction" to the little brats "seat of understanding." But that was not the approach this particular mother took. No, this mother *joined in the screaming... at the father... calling him an idiot for "not knowing that the kids always want the crust cut off!"* The outcome of such framing failure was never in doubt, and the home collapsed not many years later.

We have a dear family in the church that learned some time back the principle that the parents should never undermine the other in front of the child. After they learned it, they had the opportunity to practice it. Their son went to dad, and asked for permission to do something. Dad said no. The boy then went directly to mom, and asked her, trying to get a different answer! Her response was "Did your dad tell you no?" The boy looked dumbfounded for a moment, and finally said, "Well, yeah." The mom then replied, "Then my answer is no as well, and if you ever try anything like this again, it will be an automatic spanking!"

When children come before a spouse on the priority list, a home is framed for failure.

Genesis 2:24 *Therefore shall a man leave his father and his mother, and shall cleave unto his wife: and they shall be one flesh.*

Ephesians 5:31 *For this cause shall a man leave his father and mother, and shall be joined unto his wife, and they two shall be one flesh.* **32** *This is a great mystery: but I speak concerning Christ and the church.* **33** *Nevertheless let every one of you in particular so love his wife even as himself; and the wife see that she reverence her husband.*

Children are wonderful, precious, amazing. But what they are not, if you are biblical in your approach, is your first priority. Your first priority as a husband must be your wife, and your first priority as a wife must be your husband.

Dana and I have three wonderful children. From their earliest days, I have told them "I love you, but I love mommy most!" Mean, you say? Not at all. Let me tell you what my children have never spent a single second worrying about. They have never ever worried that mommy and daddy are splitting up. The thought has never even crossed their minds. They see mommy and daddy hug, and kiss, and flirt with each other, and they love it! My daughter Karis says, "Kiss mommy, daddy!"

Has my loving my wife more than my children, and her loving me more than the children, made them love us any less? I sincerely doubt it. Each and every day, my children subject me to multiple "hug attacks." They give me good morning kisses, good bye kisses, and good job kisses! Putting your spouse before your children will give your children the best home life imaginable. Putting your children before your spouse will produce spoiled brats, and broken homes.

When children aren't expected to obey, a home is framed for failure.

Ephesians 6:1 *Children, obey your parents in the Lord: for this is right.*

1 Samuel 15:22 *And Samuel said, Hath the LORD as great delight in burnt offerings and sacrifices, as in obeying the voice of the LORD? Behold, to obey is better than sacrifice, and to hearken than the fat of rams.*

My first job (aside from working on a farm when I was young) was at Family Dollar. I will never forget an example of how bad things can be when children are not taught to obey.

A mother came into the store one day, with a little boy in tow that appeared to be around four years old. She was there to buy household supplies, but she made the mistake of traveling through the toy aisle to get there. The boy immediately (and loudly) began to ask, then whine, and then scream for toys. When his mother ignored him, he began to reach out and grab toys by the armful, slinging some into the floor, others into the basket. The full-blown tantrum had ensued. Up one aisle, down the next, the child did as he pleased with the mother getting more and more embarrassed, but still not making the child obey or behave.

Finally, the mother got so embarrassed, she left her buggy full of items, and tried to take the child out to the car to leave. But when she got him to the door, I saw a sight I will never forget. Imagine what it would be like to try and get a four year old "Gumby" with grappling hooks on his hands and feet out of a door! The child managed to wiggle his way sideways in mommy's arms, he stuck his arms and feet straight out, and caught both sides of the doorframe. Momma pushed like a linebacker, but his flexible little body just kept springing back like a forty-pound rubber band, Sproing! Sproing! Sproing! Finally, momma reached out and, one by one, pried his little fingers (Poink! Poink! Poink! Poink!) off of the doorframe. With the last "Poink!" she finally managed to remove the child from the store.

But the battle was far from over. Unfortunately for little momma, she had parked about fifty yards from the store! Carrying that child across the parking lot took her several more minutes, with him clawing and writhing like a cat being baptized. Finally, she got him to the car, and had to enter the last phase of the battle, trying to get the child into the car. Once again, the "Gumby routine" ensued. Finally, she opened a back door, wrapped herself around the kid, crawled into the back seat with him, locked the door behind them, strapped him in, crawled out the other door, and locked that one behind her. The entire store broke into applause.

Would it not be much simpler, from their earliest days, to teach children to obey? A home has a difficult time surviving when children are not made to mind.

When parents aren't consistent and godly before their children, a home is framed for failure.

Ephesians 6:4 *And, ye fathers, provoke not your children to wrath: but bring them up in the nurture and admonition of the Lord.*

This is addressed to fathers, yes. But mothers need to take heed to it as well. If it isn't good for a father to do it, it isn't good for you to do it.

To provoke means to "exasperate, to frustrate." It indicates a parent who isn't consistently doing right, and a kid who is floundering because of it.

We had a family in our church with a daughter that "would not do right." Would we, they wondered, counsel with this girl? Of course we said that we would.

So they brought the girl, around thirteen years old, to my wife and I, and left her with us. We began to ask questions of her, probing, trying to find out where the difficulty lay, but she simply would not open up. But then came the explosion. I said to the young lady, "Why would you behave poorly, and disgrace such a godly father as you have?" At that moment, boy did she open up! She positively screamed, "My daddy is an absolute hypocrite! What you see from him here at church is the exact opposite way of how he is at home. He says "amen" here and cusses like a sailor at home. He shakes your hand here, preacher, then tells us all what a loser you are when we get in the car to leave. He acts kind here, and abuses us when no one is looking. My daddy is a two-faced liar, and if what he has is Christianity, I don't want it!

I checked. The girl was telling the truth. Little wonder then that all of the kids in the home ran as far from God as they possibly could at the first available opportunity.

PART THIRTEEN:
SIX STRAND AND CAT FIVE

A man had an independent business making deliveries to people. But one day, while delivering orders in his company truck, he ran into and injured an old lady. The lady sued and was awarded an amount large enough to drive the man out of business. After difficult times he managed to accumulate enough to try again. But a few months after opening his doors he struck and ran over an old gentleman's toe with his delivery truck. The gentleman sued and collected big damages, this time enough to ruin the man's business for good.

Later, on a peaceful Sunday afternoon, the man was sitting in his living room moping when his little boy came in and hollered "Daddy, daddy! Momma's been run over by a great big bus!"

The man's eyes absolutely filled with tears, and in a voice trembling with emotion he cried, "Thank the Lord, my luck's finally changed!"

When we got the walls framed up in the building, I went out and bought a whole bunch of two different kinds of wire. I first got about 2000 feet of six strand. That is what we used for phone wire. We have phone jacks all over that place. Then I got another 2000 or so feet of Cat Five. That is what the computers use to talk to each other, to the internet, and to the alarm system. 4000 feet of wires that no-one will ever see, but that we couldn't do without. Communication is essential to a building, and it is doubly essential to a home.

Read any book on relationships, and I can almost guarantee that the word "communication" will come up constantly. "Husbands and wives need to communicate better." "Parents and children need to communicate better." But the problem is, they don't often give you any clue how to make that happen! I can say "America needs to break it's dependence on foreign oil" all day, but unless I also say "Environmental wackos who oppose drilling on our own land here in America, Alaska, off the coast, need to be arrested for treason and gagged for life," I haven't helped you much. If you have a brain, you know that you need good communication in the home. What you may not know is how, and that's what this chapter is all about.

Don't make improving your speaking your first priority, make improving your listening your first priority.

Proverbs 18:13 *He that answereth a matter before he heareth it, it is folly and shame unto him.*

Let's translate this: he that is like about 95% of everyone you ever meet, it is folly and shame unto him!

This is true. Most people are a lot more interested in speaking than listening.

You can go to any college and find English, Spanish, Arabic, French, Swahili being taught. You can get computer programs guaranteed to have you speaking German or Finnish in just weeks. You can pick up a book, and be using sign language in no time. But when is the last time you saw a college course called "Listening 101?" When is the last time you saw a computer program that guaranteed to teach you how to speak less and hear more? When is the last time you saw a book that taught you how to speak far fewer words in a day than you do now, and dedicate that spare time to listening?

The story is told of Franklin Roosevelt, who often endured long receiving lines at the White House. He complained that no one really paid any attention to what was said. One day, during a reception, he decided to try an experiment. To each person who passed down the line and shook his hand, he murmured, "I murdered my grandmother this morning." The guests responded with phrases like, "Marvelous! Keep up the good work. We are proud of you. God bless you, sir." It was not till the end of the line, while greeting the ambassador from Bolivia, that his words were actually heard. The ambassador just leaned over and whispered, "I'm sure she had it coming."

Isn't that about how well most people listen? Everyone wants to open their mouth, but no one wants to open their ears.

You know what I have seen before? I have seen some really pretty women married to some really ugly guys. And here is the explanation I have heard more than once: *Oh, but he is such a good listener!*

But I have never, ever seen a pretty woman with an ugly guy and heard her say *Oh, but he is such a good talker!*

I'm sorry, you can talk with the voice of Barry White and be as poetic as Shakespeare, and no pretty woman is ever going to give an ugly man the time of day. But let Mr. Quasi Modo say, "Honey, why don't you tell me all about your day," and she's dragging that thing down to the Justice of the Peace on the spot.

Let a woman meet her husband at the door after he has had an awful day at work and say "baby, sit back, let me take your shoes off, and you just vent for a while, while I listen" and he is in love with her forever.

Robert W. Herron once said this: *Good listening is like tuning in a radio station. For good results, you can listen to only one station at a time. Trying to listen to my wife while looking over an office report is like trying to receive two radio stations at the same time. I end up with distortion and frustration. Listening requires a choice of where I place my attention. To tune into my partner, I must first choose to put away all that will divide my attention. That might mean laying down the newspaper, moving away from the dishes in the sink, putting down the book I'm reading, setting aside my projects.*

Listen, Listen, Listen!

Parents, this may interest you: *Teenage prostitutes, during interviews in a San Francisco study, were asked: "Is there anything you needed most and couldn't get?" Their response, invariably preceded by sadness and tears was unanimous: "What I needed most was someone to listen to me. Someone who cared enough to listen to me."*

Lecturing is all fine and good, and there is a place for it. But you know where all good communication needs to start? Not by making improving our speaking our first priority, but by making improving our listening our first priority.

A few good words are better than hours of "white noise."

Proverbs 10:19 *In the multitude of words there wanteth not sin: but he that refraineth his lips is wise.*

Ecclesiastes 5:3 *For a dream cometh through the multitude of business; and a fool's voice is known by multitude of words.*

Ecclesiastes 5:2 *Be not rash with thy mouth, and let not thine heart be hasty to utter any thing before God: for God is in heaven, and thou upon earth: therefore let thy words be few.*

As odd as it may seem, doing a whole bunch of talking is probably among the worst things you can ever do if you really want to communicate.

I remember a guy visiting here with his wife years ago, they eventually joined, then moved away, and we still love them and have contact with them. But that first day he visited, he met me by the door, and started talking to me. Twenty minutes later, everyone was gone, and he was still standing there talking to me, and I'm pretty sure he hadn't even taken a breath.

I don't even remember what he said, because after about five minutes of this, he just turned into "white noise, zzzzzzzzzzzzzzzzzz" kind of like a ballast humming on a florescent light. I like the guy to this day; he is a great guy. But you and every man in this church put together couldn't get me into a car with that guy on a long trip.

If you talk non-stop, you are not communicating, you are irritating.

Some of the greatest communicators in history have used very few words to get their point across:

On November 19, 1863, four months after Union forces defeated the Confederates at Gettysburg, the Soldiers National Cemetery at Gettysburg was dedicated. The main speaker for the day was Edward Everett, President of Harvard University, who was regarded as America's greatest orator. Mr. Everett spoke for more than two hours, and uttered 13,607 words. But I am fairly confident in saying that none of you here remember a single thing he said in all of those two hours and 13,607 words. But I bet you do remember another little speech from that day, given by a man who was only invited to speak as an afterthought. That speech went like this:

> *Four score and seven years ago our fathers brought forth on this continent a new nation, conceived in Liberty, and dedicated to the proposition that all men are created equal.*
>
> *Now we are engaged in a great civil war, testing whether that nation, or any nation, so conceived and so dedicated, can long endure. We are met on a great battlefield of that war. We have come to dedicate a portion of that field, as a final resting place for those who here gave their lives that that nation might live. It is altogether fitting and proper that we should do this.*
>
> *But, in a larger sense, we cannot dedicate — we cannot consecrate — we cannot hallow — this ground. The brave men, living and dead, who struggled here, have consecrated it, far above our poor power to add or detract. The world will little note, nor long remember what we say here, but it can never forget what they did here. It is for us the living, rather, to be dedicated here*

to the unfinished work which they who fought here have
thus far so nobly advanced. It is rather for us to be
here dedicated to the great task remaining before us —
that from these honored dead we take increased
devotion to that cause for which they gave the last full
measure of devotion — that we here highly resolve that
these dead shall not have died in vain — that this
nation, under God, shall have a new birth of freedom —
and that government of the people, by the people, for
the people, shall not perish from the earth.

It took only two minutes, and 269 words for Abraham Lincoln to have his say that day.

So which man was the better communicator? Edward Everett, with his two hour, 13, 607 word speech, or Abraham Lincoln, with his two minute, 269 word speech? That's really a no-brainer, isn't it? History has long since forgotten what Edward Everett said, but no one will ever forget the Gettysburg Address of Abraham Lincoln.

More words aren't necessarily the answer to communication. In fact, a few good words are better than hours of "white noise." If you monopolize the conversation in your home, if your spouse has to sit and listen while you rattle on, you are killing any chance you have at actual communication.

Make sure all of your words are "fitly spoken"
Proverbs 25:11 *A word fitly spoken is like apples of gold in pictures of silver.*

In other words, right words spoken in the right way are incredibly valuable! So what are words "fitly spoken?"

Fit words are words that are appropriate for the situation.
There needs to be something in you, a spiritual filter that asks "is it appropriate for me to say what I'm about to say in this particular situation?"

Maybe that time of the month when you wife feels terrible anyway isn't the time to ask when she's going on a diet...

And maybe right after your husband has been chewed out at work isn't the time to tell him what an idiot he was for leaving his old job...

Maybe the day that your wife has had it up to here with the bratty kids that you helped to produce isn't the time to say, "You don't keep the house near as clean as my momma did." You just might find yourself living in momma's clean house all over again!

Fitly spoken words are words that are appropriate for the situation.

Fit words are words that are spoken with the right tone of voice.

Honey is a great word for a spouse, unless it is spoken as **_HONEY_**!

Your tone of voice can literally ruin your marriage. I have known spouses that I considered very nearly perfect, except for the fact that they often used the harshest, most abrasive tone of voice that just ruined the entire picture. The best words in the wrong tone of voice may as well be fingernails on a blackboard.

Honey, will you puhleeze take out the trash!

Hey wife, where are my socks?

Most people give very little attention to their tone of voice. They think that they only have one voice, and they can't change it. That isn't true. The truth is, your one voice has a wide range and a lot of tones.

IT IS WITHIN MY VOICE RANGE AND TONE TO SPEAK LIKE THIS. I COULD DO IT ALL THE TIME IF I CHOSE TO.

But it's also within my voice range and tone to speak like this, and I can do it anytime I want to.

Men, ladies, listen to your own tone of voice. Tape it if you have to. Practice producing a pleasant tone of voice, it is part of "words fitly spoken."

Fit words are words that are spoken without harmful gestures.

May I demonstrate this? Even without actually saying the words, you tell me whether I am making communication easy or hard:

The first example is of an approving look and facial expression.

The second is of a negative look, rolled eyes, and hand gestures.

When you do the whole "negative gesture" thing along with the *look, we need to...* you are not speaking fit words. Fit words are words that are spoken without harmful gestures.

Fit words are words that are spoken without being incessantly negative.

I have told this story before, and will probably tell it again in the future, because I doubt seriously if I will ever encounter another living illustration quite like it:

We had a couple in church years ago. The wife was negative about everything. No matter what you said, she had a negative response. You'd go "What a pretty rainbow!" And she'd respond, "I'd rather not have to deal with all this rain!" You'd say, "What pretty leaves this fall!" And she'd say, "No-doubt we're in for an awful winter." She started off one Sunday morning, in her usual way, and I loudly said, "There's one!" A moment later, upon her second negative comment "There's two!" She said, "What are you doing?" I said, "I'm going to count out loud all of the negative comments you make today!" That fixed it, at least for the day.

How in the world do people live with Negative Nellies and Pessimist Pacos?

Husbands and wives, be careful of this. Find a way to be positive; it is part of "words fitly spoken."

Speak appropriately for the person you are speaking to.

1 Samuel 25:23 *And when Abigail saw David, she hasted, and lighted off the ass, and fell before David on her face, and bowed* *herself to the ground, 24 And fell at his feet, and said, Upon me, my lord, upon me let this iniquity be: and let thine handmaid, I pray thee, speak in thine audience, and hear the words of thine handmaid.*

Children, this means that you speak to your parents with an incredible amount of respect.

Lots of kids ought to be real happy that we are not under the law, but under grace.

Exodus 21:17 *And he that curseth his father, or his mother, shall surely be put to death.*

Leviticus 20:9 *For every one that curseth his father or his mother shall be surely put to death: he hath cursed his father or his mother; his blood shall be upon him.*

Deuteronomy 27:16 *Cursed be he that setteth light by his father or his mother. And all the people shall say, Amen.*

Proverbs 20:20 *Whoso curseth his father or his mother, his lamp shall be put out in obscure darkness.*

Under Old Testament law, if you spoke disrespectfully to your parents, you were stoned to death. Imagine that, stoned for sassing! How many of you kids are glad we aren't doing that anymore?

But it surely does let you know how God feels about it, doesn't it? Kids, your parents didn't even have to have you. They could have taken steps to make sure that they never had kids. They could have spent all the money they are spending on you on trips to the beach, on gym memberships, on new cars. If they weren't having to buy you food and clothes, they could live in a great big house with a pool.

But they chose to have you. They have worked like dogs to provide for your needs. They have spent countless nights by your bedside wiping your fevered brow. When you speak to your momma and daddy, you speak with respect. Don't call them names, don't take them lightly, you honor them when you speak to them. Yes sir, no sir, yes ma'am, no ma'am. Don't you ever let a "yeah", or "huh" or "nah" come out of your mouth to them. Speak appropriately for the person you are speaking to

Parents, this also means that you speak to your children with loving firmness.

Proverbs 1:8 *My son, hear the instruction of thy father, and forsake not the law of thy mother: 9 For they shall be an ornament of grace unto thy head, and chains about thy neck. 10 My son, if sinners entice thee, consent thou not.*

Did you see the balance here? The father was handing out commands, not suggestions. But you can also tell by what he is saying that he is concerned for his child, and is speaking in love.

Parents, speak with firmness. You are the parents; give commands. Start while they are young and when it is necessary, tell them what they are to do. It isn't always necessary; sometimes you can afford to let them make choices. But give enough commands each day (take out the trash, clean the car, straighten up your room) to keep the proper order established.

But don't forget to speak in love. If you call your kids names (stupid, dummy) then you sir, you ma'am, need to have your mouth washed out with soap. Tell your kids often that you love them. Speak to them in a kind tone of voice. If you don't, when they get old enough to go, they probably will without ever looking back.

Husbands and wives, this means that you speak to each other as one flesh.

We so often seem to forget this basic truth of marriage.

Genesis 2:24 *Therefore shall a man leave his father and his mother, and shall cleave unto his wife: and they shall be one flesh.*

Judging by how a lot of husbands and wives speak to each other, I don't think a lot of couples get that they are one flesh. If you really get that, you will speak to your spouse like you would want to be spoken to. If you get this, you will speak tenderly, kindly, lovingly. If you get this, you won't speak to each other like enemies, you will speak to each other as best friends.

Contrary to popular belief, I do have a few friends: While Buddy Dyer was working on the tile the other day, he mentioned that a mutual friend of ours, Dr. Q., was moving out to the mid-west. So I called Dr. Q. on the spot. When he answered, I said "Hey Doc, it's Brother Bo Wagner. I was just talking about you with a mutual friend of ours!"

He laughingly said, "I didn't know either of us had any friends, let alone mutual ones! I do understand that we have a lot of the same enemies, though!"

But yes, I do have quite a few friends. But you know what? My very best friend in this entire world is the woman that I am married to. We spend hours at a time talking. And we talk like friends; we talk like one flesh.

When a spouse opens up and speaks, especially on a sensitive issue, never belittle or ignore it.

1 Kings 1:16 *And Bathsheba bowed, and did obeisance unto the king. And the king said, What wouldest thou? 17 And she said unto him, My lord, thou swarest by the LORD thy God unto thine handmaid, saying, Assuredly Solomon thy son shall reign after me, and he shall sit upon my throne. 18 And now, behold, Adonijah reigneth; and now, my lord the king, thou knowest it not:*

1 Kings 1:29 *And the king sware, and said, As the LORD liveth, that hath redeemed my soul out of all distress, 30 Even as I sware unto thee by the LORD God of Israel, saying, Assuredly Solomon thy son shall reign after me, and he shall sit upon my throne in my stead; even so will I certainly do this day. 31 Then Bathsheba bowed with her face to the earth, and did reverence to the king, and said, Let my lord king David live for ever.*

Bathsheba came to her husband about one of his kids that was misbehaving. Talk about a sensitive issue! But David never one time brushed her off, he didn't belittle her, he didn't ignore what she said.

Unfortunately, what happens all too often is this: a spouse will open up and talk about something important or sensitive to them, maybe something that it is hard or embarrassing to talk about, maybe an issue in the bedroom, or a money matter, or some way that the other spouse has hurt them. And what is their reward for the effort? The other spouse either makes fun of it, or ignores it and forgets about it. That won't happen too many times before the first spouse just gives up and decides to quit even trying to talk about that issue, and probably about a lot of others as well.

Make communication a "Nike" thing: just do it!

For so many, communication is something that they say they would like to do, but they don't actually do.

Luke 15:18 *I will arise and go to my father, and will say unto him, Father, I have sinned against heaven, and before thee, **19** And am no more worthy to be called thy son: make me as one of thy hired servants. **20** And he arose, and came to his father. But when he was yet a great way off, his father saw him, and had compassion, and ran, and fell on his neck, and kissed him. **21** And the son said unto him, Father, I have sinned against heaven, and in thy sight, and am no more worthy to be called thy son.*

This young man <u>decided</u> to communicate, and then he went and <u>did it.</u> I dare say that many of you out there right now have been thinking, "You know, I really need to talk to my spouse more. You know, I really need to spend time connecting with the kids" but you just haven't done it. I have two words for you: do it! It may be awkward at first. You may have to start with "So, enjoying all this hot weather?" Whatever it takes, just start it, just do it.

I have had the privilege of doing a whole lot of marriage counseling over the years. And when a couple in trouble comes to see me, one of my first goals is to get them together, in my office, where I can make sure that everybody keeps a level head and a pleasant tone of voice, and actually get them talking. Good things tend to start at that point.

Do you want to know how seriously God takes this thing of communication? Look at what He calls Himself:

John 1:1 *In the beginning was the **Word**, and the **Word** was with God, and the Word was God.*

Do you want to know how seriously God takes this thing of communication? Look at what Hebrews 1 says:

Hebrews 1:1 *God, who at sundry times and in divers manners* **spake** *in time past unto the fathers by the prophets,* **2a** *Hath in these last days* **spoken** *unto us by his Son...*

Maybe it's time to check up on the six strand and cat five in your home.

P.S to Dana: SHMILY!

PART FOURTEEN:
O LORD SEND THE HIGH VOLTAGE, 3 PHASE, 600 AMP POWER JUST NOW

In the mid 1970s, a young man in Taiwan fell madly in love with a young lady, and determined to convince her to marry him. His plan was to write and mail her love letters till she fell for him. So between 1974 and 1976, he wrote and mailed more than 700 mushy letters to his intended bride. He told her how lovely her eyes were, and how beautiful her hair was, and how smooth her skin was, and how she just made his heart sing, and how he couldn't live without her, and how he was going to make her the happiest woman alive. After two years, and more than 700 letters, the girl finally fell in love and agreed to be married... to the mailman that delivered all of those 700 letters!

One of my concerns when we began to plan for the new building was the electrical. I've done a lot of residential electrical, but not much on the commercial scale. And even the stuff I initially did at the first little church building had some "interesting moments."

I remember that I needed to cut into a wire up in the attic to get power for some new lights. I located every wire coming into the light box that I was working near. There were four of them coming out of the junction box. I traced them all down. Three went out to other lights, one went back to the breaker box. I cut off the breaker to that wire. Confident that I had taken proper precautions, I picked one of the three remaining wires to cut into for my power source. I got my lineman pliers, put them on the wire, squeezed real hard, and POW! I melted the jaws of those big pliers; the flash was so bright I couldn't even see for the next minute or so.

When I got my sight back and stopped shaking, I was not happy. I had cut off the power going into that box, and still cut a live wire coming out. That ought to be impossible.   I went back to that junction box, and started poking around. When I did, I found out that the box wasn't mounted flush against the drywall. It was sitting about a half inch up off of it, it had no cover, and someone had run another power wire into it through the front, and hooked it up to the wire that I had cut.

Needless to say, we were excited about getting a new electrical system to go along with our new building!

Still, when I got the plans back from the architect and looked at the electrical pages, complete with 3 phase power, 600 amps worth of breakers, and the most complex diagram I've ever seen, I knew it was beyond my ability to do alone. But a very good God had already provided Brother Eddie to us!

So he and I went to work. We spent about six weeks bending and hanging conduit. We mounted hundreds of outlet boxes, and that was just in Mrs. Dana's office! (After being confined to an office with only one outlet for all these years, she deserves it.)

We put two of the biggest breaker boxes you can imagine on the back wall. We crawled up on lifts and pulled 10-14 wires at a time through those pipes. We flexed wires into impossible places. We routed and re-routed circuits. We planned out multiple switch capabilities for major areas. And we still aren't even done yet!

Why in the world are we doing all that work? Why not just skip that part so we can get into the building earlier? Because for some reason, a big beautiful church building with no power for lights, air conditioning, heating, water heaters, sound boards, and things like that, just isn't going to be a very good building! A good building needs power.

A home without power makes about as much sense as a building without power. If your home is ever going to be what it should be, it is going to have to have the power of God coursing through it.

People seem to have at least some understanding of the fact that the power of God should be present in church. They seem to know that things work better, more people are saved, more people do right, and there are less struggles and strife when the power of God is present.

But you aren't in church 24 hours a day. You are, however, in a family 24 hours a day. You dads are dads all day every day. You moms are moms all day every day. You husbands are husbands all day every day. You wives are wives all day every day. You kids are your parent's children all day every day. If it is important for the power of God to be present during the four or five hours a week that you are in church, how much more important is it that the power of God be present during the 168 hours a week that you are in a family?

A secular counselor will never say this, because he or she cannot even begin to understand it. But you better understand it. The God who invented the family must also empower the family if that family is to thrive. A family may possibly survive without the power of God, but it will never, ever, ever thrive without the power of God.

I will go so far as to say this: if you put all of the other practical things that I have taught you in this book into practice in your home; the financial things, the intimate things, the communication tools, and so on, yet you don't have the power of God in your home, you are still a home at great risk of failure. Your home needs the power of God..

Before I even begin to tell you how to have the power of God in your home, let me take just a few moments and tell you why you need it and what it can do for you.

The power of God in your home will help to save the souls of your children.

Acts 16:25 *And at midnight Paul and Silas prayed, and sang praises unto God: and the prisoners heard them. 26 And suddenly there was a great earthquake, so that the foundations of the prison were shaken: and immediately all the doors were opened, and every one's bands were loosed. 27 And the keeper of the prison awaking out of his sleep, and seeing the prison doors open, he drew out his sword, and would have killed himself, supposing that the prisoners had been fled. 28 But Paul cried with a loud voice, saying, Do thyself no harm: for we are all here. 29 Then he called for a light, and sprang in, and came trembling, and fell down before Paul and Silas, 30 And brought them out, and said, Sirs, what must I do to be saved?*

When Paul and Silas found themselves in prison, everyone there found themselves under the sound of the gospel. The seed was planted. But when the power of God fell, that seed sprang to life and the jailer himself got saved!

You absolutely need to keep your kids under the sound of the gospel. But if you keep them under the sound of the gospel and combine it with the power of God in your own home, your children will most likely get saved. If conviction just falls on them here, they can hold out till they get home and get out from under it, and eventually get hardened to it. But if they fall under conviction here, and there is so much power of God in your own home that that conviction follows them into the front door, and down the hall, and into their bedroom, and under the covers with them, those kids will probably get saved.

Life in a home is much, much easier with a bunch of truly saved kids, especially when those kids get to be teenagers!

The power of God in your home will help to protect you from deterioration from within.

Psalm 18:32 *It is God that girdeth me with strength, and maketh my way perfect. 33 He maketh my feet like hinds' feet, and setteth me upon my high places.*

Hind is the Bible word for deer. David said that God would give him strength, power, and that when He did, he would be like a deer scaling the cliffs. In other words, life would be anything but boring, dull, monotonous, and unpleasant.

Outward dangers like pornography, adultery, booze, and things like them, do destroy homes. But lots of homes, rather than exploding, simply deteriorate from within.

Pastors get to counsel with a lot of "surprise" break ups, people that have been together for twenty, thirty years or more, showed no signs of problems, yet ended up breaking up. It wasn't an explosion that got them, it was deterioration, the very deterioration that the power of God would have prevented. Good things just don't deteriorate in the presence of the power of God. When you have a man and wife on fire for God, and empowered by God, there will be an excitement in the home that keeps things from deteriorating.

It is fun to watch old couples, still on fire for God, because those couples will also still be madly in love with each other.

The power of God will help to protect you from temptations from without.

Matthew 6:13 *And lead us not into temptation, but deliver us from evil: For thine is the kingdom, and the power, and the glory, forever. Amen.*

In the same verse that tells us to pray that we not be led into temptation and that we be delivered from evil, we read of the power of God. That is not accidental, for it is only the power of God that can keep us from those things.

Make no mistake about it, this is a world filled with temptations, and those devil-made temptations are designed to ruin homes. You need the power of God to protect you.

Now let's look at some ways to bring that glorious power into your home.

God's indwelling power will only come to people who are truly born again.

Acts 4:7 *And when they had set them in the midst, they asked, By what power, or by what name, have ye done this? 8 Then Peter, filled with the Holy Ghost, said unto them, Ye rulers of the people, and elders of Israel, 9 If we this day be examined of the good deed done to the impotent man, by what means he is made whole; 10 Be it known unto you all, and to all the people of Israel, that by the name of Jesus Christ of Nazareth, whom ye crucified, whom God raised from the dead, even by him doth this man stand here before you whole.*

Peter, a born-again Christian, healed a lame man. The rulers wanted to know what power he did it by, because they themselves, lost men, never for a moment had that kind of power. Peter, a saved man, did.

If you aren't saved, for the sake of your soul, and for the sake of your home, you need to get <u>truly</u> saved.

God's power will come as we consciously desire and seek after it.

2 Kings 2:14 *And he took the mantle of Elijah that fell from him, and smote the waters, and said, Where is the LORD God of Elijah? and when he also had smitten the waters, they parted hither and thither: and Elisha went over.*

For Elisha, the power of God was not an "accidental thing." It did not simply happen at random, he sought after it. The same must be true of us. You eat what you hunger for, you find what you look for, you receive what you ask for.

God's power will come as we set ourselves apart from sin.

Ezra 6:21 *And the children of Israel, which were come again out of captivity, and all such as had separated themselves unto them* *from the filthiness of the heathen of the land, to seek the LORD God of Israel, did eat,* **22** *And kept the feast of unleavened bread seven days with joy: for the LORD had made them joyful, and turned the heart of the king of Assyria unto them, to strengthen their hands in the work of the house of God, the God of Israel.*

In verse twenty-one, the people separated and purified themselves. It was then, in verse twenty-two, that God "strengthened their hands."

I preached a family conference a few years ago for Gary Gibson, a wonderful preacher friend of mine in the Lexington area. While we were there, he took us on a tour of one of the major NASCAR racing shops. It was like absolutely nothing I had ever seen. My experience with "automotive shops" had given me a stereotypical view of a place that is dirty, greasy, oily, untidy. But when I stood on the second floor observation deck, looking through a huge pane of glass down into the engine shop, I was amazed at what I saw. All of the mechanics were wearing scrubs, like surgeons, complete with masks. The floor was so gleaming and shiny you could have licked it and not worried about a single germ. There were huge filters, removing every speck of dust from the air. When I asked the tour guide why it was like this, he explained, "In NASCAR, races can be won or lost by 1/1000 of an inch. And a speck of dust in the engine can be the very thing that makes you 1/1000 of an inch behind, instead of 1/1000 of an inch ahead. Our drivers aren't going to lose a race because a speck of dirt or dust robbed them of their power." Oh, that God's people fully understood this principle! God's power flows best through purity!

God's power will come as we spend time isolated alone with Him.

Exodus 34:27 *And the LORD said unto Moses, Write thou these words: for after the tenor of these words I have made a covenant with thee and with Israel.* **28** *And he was there with the LORD forty days and forty nights; he did neither eat bread, nor drink water. And* *he wrote upon the tables the words of the covenant, the ten commandments. 29 And it came to pass, when Moses came down from mount Sinai with the two tables of testimony in Moses' hand, when he came down from the mount, that Moses wist not that the skin of his face shone while he talked with him. 30 And when Aaron and all the children of Israel saw Moses, behold, the skin of his face shone; and they were afraid to come nigh him. 31 And Moses called unto them; and Aaron and all the rulers of the congregation returned unto him: and Moses talked with them. 32 And afterward all the children of Israel came nigh: and he gave them in commandment all that the LORD had spoken with him in mount Sinai. 33 And till Moses had done speaking with them, he put a vail on his face. 34 But when Moses went in before the LORD to speak with him, he took the vail off, until he came out. And he came out, and spake unto the children of Israel that which he was commanded. 35 And the children of Israel saw the face of Moses, that the skin of Moses' face shone: and Moses put the vail upon his face again, until he went in to speak with him.*

Forty *days* alone with God is a very long time. But if you are going to spend forty *years* in the wilderness, it will be forty days well spent! You have no idea what lies ahead in your life, or your home. The best thing you can do is prepare for the worst, by spending so much alone time with God that you are empowered for whatever comes your way.

Power, power, power, the Christian home must have the power of God to survive and thrive!

PART FIFTEEN:
1400 REASONS I CAN NO LONGER
SEE THROUGH WALLS

In a story called "The Oval Portrait," Edgar Alan Poe tells the story of an injured man who stopped at an abandoned old castle in the woods. He and his servant got inside, and bedded down in one of the smaller rooms. That room had paintings all over the walls, good paintings. There was a book on the nightstand that gave the names of the paintings and the stories behind them. The man was reading them by candlelight, while his servant had drifted off to sleep nearby. The man's eyes were getting tired, so he moved the candelabra closer. When he did, it lit up a part of the wall that had been shrouded in darkness. In that spot was a painting that for some reason made the man immediately close his eyes tight.

He knew that was an odd reaction, and sitting there with his eyes closed, he could not figure out why he had done it. Slowly he opened them again, and looked at the picture once more. It was of a girl, just blossoming into womanhood. She was stunningly beautiful, but that was not what made the picture so unnerving. As he stared and studied it, he could not shake the feeling that the painting was alive, even though he knew it was not.

Picking up the book, he flipped to the page that told the story of the painting. The painting was of the bride of the artist himself. She loved life, loved fun, loved being happy, but more than all of that, she loved her husband the artist.

He, though, had only one great love, and that was art itself. His art became a rival for her affection, till she dreaded seeing him put brush to canvas. One day, her worst nightmare came true, when he determined to paint a portrait of her. But dutifully, she complied. Day after day for countless silent hours, she sat in the tower, away from the sun, while he painted her by candlelight. The more he painted, the more excited he became about what he was producing. He was meticulous, accurately capturing every detail, yet missing the one detail that he needed to see; his young bride's health was suffering from the long hours of sitting indoors in that drafty castle.

Yet the artist painted on. Feverishly, furiously, he painted. Weeks passed into months, and it was as if a madness had possessed him. The painting was the masterpiece of the ages, and he must complete it, and it must be perfect.

And finally it was done. The last brush stroke crossed the canvas, the artist stepped back and gazed at it approvingly, and shouted, "This is life indeed!" just as his young bride was breathing her last earthly breath. He saw all the things he didn't need to see, and missed all of the things he did need to see.

That illustration sits so well with the truth I want to examine in this chapter.

After we got all of the framing done, and all of the wires run, we could look around on a very unique sight. I could stand in the middle of the auditorium, turn around in a slow circle, and see right into six Sunday School rooms, the janitors closet, the bathrooms, the vestibule, the cry room, both nurseries, every hallway, and all four offices. I could literally see through every wall in the entire building.

That had to change. We just could not have a church where people could see through the walls of one room into every other room. The same thing is true when you build a house. How awkward would it be living in a home where you could see through the bare stud walls into every bedroom, every bathroom, every single room of the house? That would be a classic case of TMI; Too Much Information.

No, those bare stud walls needed to be covered. And so we hung drywall. And hung drywall, and hung drywall, and hung drywall, and hung drywall, and hung drywall.

> *We hung drywall from the floor, and off of ladders and over doors, we hung it high, we hung it low, up on lifts, away we'd go!*
>
> *Four by twelve, not four by eight, 5/8th inch, oh feel the weight! Double sided, six layers tall, got to have a firewall!*
>
> *All the way up to the ceiling, back is breaking, what a feeling! Before I'd hang another sheet, I'd find Green Eggs And Ham to eat!*

I think I am safe in saying that those of us who spent all those months hanging those 1400 plus sheets of drywall are really glad that we're done hanging the drywall.

But you know what? We needed to have that drywall covering those stud walls. We just don't need to see from room to room. It wouldn't cause anything but trouble for every Sunday School teacher and student to be looking through the walls at the other classes of teachers and students who are looking into the nursery at the babies and workers who are looking into the offices. We just don't need to see everything.

As amazing as it sounds, the same thing is true of a good home. There needs to be some things that we intentionally try not to see!

This seems counterintuitive. We tend to think that if you know everything and see everything, you must be better off. But truthfully, the best homes are homes where people intentionally choose not to "see" some things.

Choose not to see "the glories of life before you got married"

You know what I really love? I love seeing that look of shock that comes over a newlyweds face after about a month when they finally realize how drastically their life has changed. Newsflash: married and single are from two different galaxies. Even Paul mentioned some of the differences:

1 Corinthians 7:32 *But I would have you without carefulness. He that is unmarried careth for the things that belong to the Lord, how he may please the Lord: 33 But he that is married careth for the things that are of the world, how he may please his wife. 34 There is difference also between a wife and a virgin. The unmarried woman careth for the things of the Lord, that she may be holy both in body and in spirit: but she that is married careth for the things of the world, how she may please her husband.*

Oh yes, there is a great big difference between married and single. And here is where a problem comes in. There truly is something glorious about "single!" I mean the memories of those good old "footloose and fancy-free" days.

Do you remember when you had all that money to spend, and almost no bills?

Do you remember when you could pick up and go off for a few days on the spur of the moment?

But those aren't really the big ones. You know the ones that are really dangerous? The ones where the husband looks at his wife, and then his mind drifts back to all those other girls that wanted him before he got "snagged."

And the wife, she sees her low/middle income husband, and her mind drifts back to that guy she could have married who was such a moneymaker.

You need about 1400 sheets of 5/8th inch drywall in front of that memory. You don't even need to see them, for several good reasons:

The only thing you ever tend to remember about the "good old days" is the good. But in reality, there was a whole lot of bad that went along with all that good!

Even the good parts of the past can never be regained, and focusing on the past completely robs you of the joy of the present, so choose not to see "the glories of life before you got married!

Choose not to see "gender specific" irritants

When I do marriage counseling with a prospective couple, let me show you one of the first things I point out to them:

Genesis 2:18 *And the LORD God said, It is not good that the man should be alone; I will make him an* **help meet** *for him. 19 And out of the ground the LORD God formed every beast of the field, and every fowl of the air; and brought them unto Adam to see what he would call them: and whatsoever Adam called every living creature, that was the name thereof. 20 And Adam gave names to all cattle, and to the fowl of the air, and to every beast of the field; but for Adam there was not found an* **help meet** *for him.*

What is a "help meet?" Basically, it is a counterpart, an opposite piece of the puzzle to help complete the whole picture. In other words, God took everything that man was, and made woman the opposite. That is what makes it so creepy when you see a guy acting "girlie."

A woman doing that would not attract any notice at all. A girl can be into pocketbooks, and craft stores, and pumps, and it's no big deal.

The opposite is also true. Because God made men and women exactly opposite, it is creepy beyond measure when you see some woman in Big Boy Biker Britches with the wallet attached by a steel chain, chawin' on a wad of backy, and takin' on all comers in a belchin' contest.

God designed men and women to be different. And when you get married, you will find the differences to be wonderful, most of the time.

But humans are humans, and, inevitably, we always tend to think people that aren't like us are just a little irritating. And so, the "gender specific irritants" begin to gnaw away at us.

When the phone rings, 95% of the time do you know what a man's number one priority is? To get that call over with as soon as possible. Why? Because he's a man, that's why. The woman? If my sister-in-law calls, plan on talking for at least a half hour, even if she called you by accident. Why? She's a woman; it's in her genetic makeup, so just get over it.

Men are loud. They have big lungs. They have big mouths. They like noise. Get over it; it's a man thing.

Women are emotional. They cry a lot. Sometimes even they themselves have no idea why (that is always fun). It's a woman thing (it sure would be odd if it were a man thing!) Just get over it.

A man in a new outfit, if there is something broken somewhere nearby, even if he really doesn't know how to fix it, is going to crawl under it in those new clothes and poke around, just because there are grease blobs and cool tools involved. It's what we do, don't ask why; it just is.

A woman will get mad at you if you do something wrong in her dreams. (I know what I am talking about. When you wake up in the morning and your wife is glaring at you and you say, "What's wrong" and she says, "Nothing!" You know it's going to be an interesting day.)

Why would a woman get mad over something in a dream? Because she's a woman, that's all you need to know.

Men are big and clumsy and they leave things lying around and they make messes and they're stubborn. Amen, ladies?

Ladies are unpredictable and emotional and obsessive compulsive about the smallest things and prone to mood swings. Amen, men?

And you know what? You need a bunch of drywall on those bare stud walls to keep you from even seeing all of that from day to day. God made you different, and the little irritants are just part of the package deal. That big clumsy oaf sure is nice to have around when a jar needs opening, or a tire needs changing, or when the creep down the street needs to be punched out.

That emotional, erratic woman sure is nice to have around come suppertime, and bedtime, and "I have the flu, will you please baby me" time.

Choose not to see unchangeable physical "flaws," or the natural effects of aging.

Here is a neat truth: if you are right with God, there will be a lot of your spouse-to-be that you never see until you get married. People who undress people they are not married to are not right with God.

So when you get married, you get the joy of discovery. And what you discover will be a physically imperfect human being. There is no physically perfect human being on earth; we all have what could be called "physical flaws." (Not you, Dana, you are obviously the exception).

And it only gets worse as we age. Age does weird things to our bodies. We spot and scar and sag and wrinkle and expand and droop and gray and on and on. The Bible itself has a picturesque passage describing this:

Ecclesiastes 12:1 *Remember now thy Creator in the days of thy youth, while the evil days come not, nor the years draw nigh, when thou shalt say, I have no pleasure in them; 2 While the sun, or the light, or the moon, or the stars, be not darkened, nor the clouds return after the rain: 3 In the day when the keepers of the house shall **tremble (the hands start to shake)**, and the strong men shall bow themselves **(The legs get feeble and weak)**, and the grinders cease because they are few **(not many teeth left)** , and those that look out of the windows be darkened **(failing eyesight, probably need glasses)** , 4 And the* *doors shall be shut in the streets, when the sound of the grinding is low* **(you have to keep your lips tight together when eating because there are not many teeth left and you don't want food falling out)** *, and he shall rise up at the voice of the bird* **(can't help waking up early)** *, and all the daughters of musick shall be brought low* **(start to lose range and strength of voice)** *; 5 Also when they shall be afraid of that which is high* **(might fall and break a hip or something else)** *, and fears shall be in the way* **(scared to go out, not much strength left to handle danger)** *, and the almond tree shall flourish* **(hair turns gray or white)** *, and the grasshopper shall be a burden* **(can't lift much)** *, and desire shall fail* **(not interested in things that used to be pleasurable)**...

Yes, people do have natural physical flaws, and yes, age changes people.

A wise old sage once gave some very good advice: keep both eyes wide open before marriage, and one completely closed afterward.

Now let me say a few things here. It is essential that we keep ourselves as fit and attractive as possible for the person we are married to. When you see a person who can't squeeze into the booth at the buffet restaurant with their usual five-pound plate of food that has produced a 550-pound posterior, that is not a "natural flaw" or an "effect of aging." We need to treat God and our spouses better than that.

But when a person is who God made them to be physically, and the spouse who married them starts giving them a hard time about their nose, or their birthmark, or their forehead, that spouse needs an attitude adjustment.

And when a young couple marries, and grows old together, there is something wicked and worthless about one spouse giving the other fits over the natural effects of aging. Again, do everything you can to maintain a healthy, youthful appearance as long as you can. Don't adopt the "granny look" in your forties, or do the "grandpa pants" in your youth." But folks, there is nothing but glory in the natural effects of aging:

186

Proverbs 16:31 *The hoary head is a crown of glory, if it be found in the way of righteousness.*

White hair has a beauty all it's own. Those lines around the eyes from a lifetime of laughing together can be a beautiful thing.

Some years back, a 60-year-old man who had been married for 40 years starred in a movie called "Crocodile Dundee." Shortly thereafter, he left his wife of 40 years for his co-star of 20+ years younger. How wicked!

How wicked when a man spends a lifetime working in the factory, getting scars and wrinkles and rough and calloused hands, only to have a wife despise those things.

How wicked when a woman goes to death's door to deliver three or four of a man's children, then loses sleep for the next 20 years raising them, and then that man leaves because his wife no longer looks like the girl he married.

Let me remind you of a few things:

That spouse in whom you have noticed physical flaws has also noticed some physical flaws in you. You better give the same mercy you hope to receive.

If your spouse were any more perfect, he or she probably wouldn't have married you to start with!

That spouse who is flawed, or is growing old, is a person that God created, and loved, and died for, and you need to treat him/her very carefully.

There is nothing better, nothing more comfortable, than marrying someone, loving them, living with them flaws and all, till you grow old together and then death do you part, and then you eventually reunite on the streets of gold in your new, glorified bodies!

So for those physical flaws and natural effect of aging, choose not to see them. Put up 1400 sheets of 5/8th inch in the way.

Choose not to see the things that have made you angry or hurt in the past.

While working on the building yesterday, Buddy Dyer asked me what I thought was the main killer of homes. With little hesitation at all, I said, "unforgiveness."

There is one thing that everyone eventually needs, and that is forgiveness over something. When that forgiveness does not come, a home is well on the way to be ruined. Listen to a very convicting passage:

Matthew 6:14 *For if ye forgive men their trespasses, your heavenly Father will also forgive you: 15 But if ye forgive not men their trespasses, neither will your Father forgive your trespasses.*

More and more, I am questioning the sanity of people. People that would rather harbor bitterness than forgive, even while that very bitterness is destroying them and their home, have got to be a little crazy.

Even secular magazines give testimony to the necessity for forgiveness. One night, Dana fell asleep with "Better Homes and Gardens" there on the bed. I picked it up and started thumbing through it. Guys, trust me on this one, unless you are interested in absolute nothingness, don't waste your time. That is definitely one of those "women are different from men" kind of things.

But in that magazine, there was an article on the necessity of forgiveness! The writer made the statement "forgiveness isn't even for the benefit of the person you are forgiving; it is for your benefit." It sounds like that writer had read Matthew 6:14-15!

Forgiveness truly is for your benefit. Science has proven that there are health benefits to forgiving. Everything from lower blood pressure, to less mental problems, to lower instance of ulcers, and on and on.

Forgiveness will make a spouse love you more than ever. We love Jesus because of what He forgave us for!

One day, two monks were walking through the countryside. They were on their way to another village to help bring in the crops. As they walked, they spied an old woman sitting at the edge of a river. She was upset because there was no bridge, and she could not get

188

across on her own. The first monk kindly offered, "We will carry you across if you would like." "Thank you," she said gratefully, accepting their help. So the two men joined hands, lifted her between them and carried her across the river. When they got to the other side, they set her down, and she went on her way.

After they had walked another mile or so, the second monk began to complain. "Look at my clothes," he said. "They are filthy from carrying that woman across the river. And my back still hurts from lifting her. I can feel it getting stiff." The first monk just smiled and nodded his head.

A few more miles up the road, the second monk griped again, "My back is hurting me so badly, and it is all because we had to carry that silly woman across the river! I cannot go any farther because of the pain." The first monk looked down at his partner, now lying on the ground, moaning. "Have you wondered why I am not complaining?" he asked. "Your back hurts because you are still carrying the woman. But I set her down five miles ago."

That is what many of us are like in dealing with our families. We are that second monk who cannot let go. We hold the pain of the past over our loved ones' heads like a club, or we remind them every once in a while, when we want to get the upper hand, of the burden we still carry because of something they did years ago.

Let it go! If you really, really, really want a great marriage, forgive everything done to you, let it go, and choose not to see it any more.

Isaiah 38:17 *Behold, for peace I had great bitterness: but thou hast in love to my soul delivered it from the pit of corruption: for thou hast cast all my sins behind thy back.*

That is a picturesque way of saying "God puts our sins where He cannot look at them anymore! We need to do the same.

How many marriages are like an obsessed artist, who sees all of the things he doesn't need to see, and misses all of the things he does.

PART SIXTEEN:
HVAC: TONS OF CORRECTION, PLEASANT RESULTS

Nine men and one woman had gotten trapped in their different vehicles in a sudden flood. All of them got out, up onto the top of their cars, and screamed for help, as the floodwaters rose ever higher. Just in time, the local rescue helicopter came flying in, with a rope dangling for the nine men and one woman to catch and hold on to so the copter could carry them to safety. One by one, all ten grabbed hold of the rope. But as the helicopter began to carry them over the water to safety, the pilot quickly realized that ten people hanging on was one person too many, and that he was not going to make it unless one of them let go. So he shouted down to them "We're one person too heavy! One of you is going to have to let go for the good of all the others.

Sadly, all of the men behaved like little boys. They began to whine and moan about why they needed to be the one to hang on, and why someone else needed to let go. Finally, the one woman spoke up. She said, "I'll do it. I'm a wife, and a mom, and a volunteer with Hospice, so everything I do is a sacrifice for others. I'll be willing to sacrifice myself once more so that all of you can live."

The nine men hanging onto the rope were so moved by her speech, that they all began to clap.

God has been so good to us in this building project. When we began planning for it, I took the blueprints around to a bunch of different places to get quotes on supplies. When it came to the HVAC system (heating, ventilation, air conditioning) we were in for a serious case of sticker shock. The most reasonable quote we got for a turnkey job was $94,500! But then God sent a good preacher friend of mine by. He just happened to know a very unusual gentleman. This gentleman at the time owned an HVAC manufacturing firm, and loved the King James Bible. Why do I mention those two things together? Because for churches that take a firm stand on the KJV, he provided HVAC units at manufacturers cost. If you weren't a real live KJV church, he wouldn't even talk to you. He provided all of our units for us, another good local brother, James Jones of Jones Heating and Air got us into the CC Dixon wholesale supply house, and when it is all said and done, we are going to have about $30,000 in our HVAC system, for a savings of about $65,000 dollars. Wonderfully for us, sadly for others, that dear HVAC manufacturer is now retired.

In doing a lot of HVAC homework, I have learned some unusual things. For instance, air conditioners do not produce cold and put it into the air, they remove heat from the air. Nor do heat pumps produce heat and put it into the air, they remove coolness from the air. In both instances, the air in the room is sucked into the unit, and put under tremendous pressure. Then when the air is properly corrected the way you want it, it is sent back into the inside air handler and distributed throughout the rooms.

That air comes into the unit "natural." It leaves the unit "corrected." No one really wants "natural" air, because the natural, about 95% of the time, is either too hot or too cold.

And this is where we will begin to make all of our church children very nervous, because what I am getting at is the issue of child discipline, otherwise known in these here parts as "whoopins."

See, about 95% of the time, "natural" in kids is not good. We are after "corrected" kids. Let's look at Proverbs 19:18 for our text on this subject.

Proverbs 19:18 *Chasten thy son while there is hope, and let not thy soul spare for his crying.*

There is a commercial series out about milk. It will show some guy or girl drinking a tall glass of milk, and then putting the glass down and smiling, with a big ol' milk mustache. It's theme is *Milk: it does a body good!* I'm sure it probably does. It has calcium, vitamin d, and many other helpful things. But I tell you the commercial series I would like to see. It would show some kid smart off at mom or dad. Then it would show that kid bending over a bed, while daddy swings a paddle into his rear end. And then while the kid is hopping around howling and holding his tail, dad would look at the camera and smile and say *Spanking: it does a body good!*

This is not nearly the same world that we used to live in. Violent crime is going through the roof. Kids are bringing guns to school and shooting the place up. Young people have little or no respect for teachers, principal, parents, employers, pastors, or adults in general. And let me tell you the main difference between how things used to be and how they are now: the difference is, adults used to understand the value of a good old fashioned spanking!

Spankings have always been hated by kids, but now, dumb adults in positions of power and influence hate them too. Psychologists try to convince us that spanking will "warp a child's psyche." Teachers tell kids who have been spanked to report their parents to DSS. TV newscasters do report after report, talking to all kinds of "experts" that all agree that spankings are old fashioned and out of date. Judges try to jail parents who still spank their kids, or preachers who still believe what the Bible says about spanking. And the more that adults forsake the Bible teaching of spankings, the more schools that ban corporal punishment, the more out of control the bad kids of today become. If you are going to build a good home, child discipline must be part of it. Let's look at this thought.

Spanking is a sign that a parent loves a child

Proverbs 3:11 *My son, despise not the chastening of the LORD; neither be weary of his correction:* **12** *For whom the LORD loveth he correcteth; even as a father the son in whom he delighteth.*

God Himself spanks His children. We may not be able to see the paddle, but He does use it. Sometimes it may be a sickness, or sometimes a ticket, or something breaking down, but God does swing the paddle on His disobedient children. The New Testament bears this out.

Hebrews 12:6 *For whom the Lord loveth he chasteneth, and scourgeth every son whom he receiveth.* **7** *If ye endure chastening, God dealeth with you as with sons; for what son is he whom the father chasteneth not?* **8** *But if ye be without chastisement, whereof all are partakers, then are ye bastards, and not sons.*

God loves His children enough to spank them. And Proverbs 3:12 compares a father who spanks his son to God who spanks His children. Both are motivated by love.

Trust me on this, it hurts a parent's heart really, really bad, to have to spank a child. So why do we do it? Because we love our kids enough to care about how they behave, and how they turn out. Verse twelve says that a father who spanks his son *delights* in him (and it applies to daughters also). There are no kids on earth that I love more than Caleb, Karis, and Aléthia. Yet I spank every one of them! Why? Because I love them, and I see the benefits that spanking gives to them.

Experts tell us just to "hold reasonable conversations" with our children.

Before my kids could hold a "reasonable conversation" with me, I taught them not to gouge each other's eyes. How? Every time they tried it, they got a swat. Before my kids could hold a "reasonable conversation" with me, I taught them not to shove food off the table into the floor. How? Every time they tried it, they got a swat. Before my kids could hold a "reasonable conversation" with me, I taught them

194

not to spit on each other. How? Every time they tried it, they got a swat. I love them enough to do whatever is necessary to ensure that they grow up well mannered and well behaved. They can't always understand what I say, but they do understand that when they do something, and it results in their tail hurting or the back of their hand hurting, they should stop doing whatever it was that caused their tail or the back of their hand to hurt!

I am really big into "behavioral modification," and there is no better tool to accomplish that than a spanking paddle! If you want to raise thugs and brats, help yourself. But I have a few thousand years of historical practice and several hundred verses of Scripture to let me know that if I want to raise good kids, spanking is going to have to be a part of the process! If you really love your kids, you will spank them when they need it.

Parents who don't spank their children when they need it are actually guilty of hating their children!

This is not my opinion; this is God's Word:

Proverbs 13:24 *He that spareth his rod hateth his son: but he that loveth him chasteneth him betimes.*

Parents often refuse to spank their children, and say "I love them too much to spank them." That is a lie. A lie, a lie, a lie, a big fat hairy lie with sweaty armpits. The truth is, if a parent refuses to spank their kids, they hate them. If they didn't, they would love them enough to spank them when they need it. ***Parents who refuse to spank their kids love themselves, not their kids.***

They love themselves too much to endure hearing their children cry.

They love themselves too much to have their kids wheel around and glare at them and say, "I hate you!"

They love themselves too much to try and break their children's stubborn will.

After a spanking, our kids have, a few times, done the "I hate you" thing. Our answer is always the same. "That's fine, hate me all

195

you like. But I love you enough to demand that you do right, and to punish you when you don't."

Spanking helps to remove the natural foolishness that a child is born with.

Proverbs 22:15 *Foolishness is bound in the heart of a child; but the rod of correction shall drive it far from him.*

Kids do not come into this world as pure as the wind driven snow, and then suddenly, when the terrible two's start, change and end up needing spankings. Children, sweet loveable cuddly children are born with a sin nature; they are born with foolishness bound up in their heart. You may not really be able to see it until the terrible twos begin, but it is there. And as soon as it starts to show itself, you need to know that the rod of correction will be necessary to remove it.

By the way, the rod is a somewhat general term to this discussion. The rod may actually end up being a paint stick, a wooden spoon, a paddle, whatever is **safe** and **effective**.

A friend of ours had an eleven-month-old crawler. She had just mopped the kitchen floor. Little crawler started to crawl out onto it, and momma firmly said "No." Little crawler looked at her, and started out onto it. She picked him up, and moved him back into the other room, pointed at the wet floor, and again gave a firm "No." Little crawler tried again. Again he was moved, and again, told "No." By this point, it was obvious that little crawler knew beyond any doubt that he was not to go onto the wet floor, and was determined to do it anyway. So when he started onto it for the third time, Momma added a pop on the hand to her "No." The kid wailed, and momma put him down in the other room again. He started right back onto the wet floor, and was again met with a no and a pop on the hand. This happened 8 times! But after the eighth time, little crawler didn't try it any more, ***and from that point on, when momma told him not to go somewhere, he obeyed!*** That is going to come in very handy when little crawler turns sixteen.

196

Can you imagine what life we would be like with a teenager who never had the natural foolishness of a toddler spanked out of them? I mean a teenager who would stomp their foot, scream, throw tantrums? I know that some of you can imagine it, because you are either living it, or you know people who are living it. Sorry, there is no re-wind button on life.

Spankings should always be spankings, never abuse.

Proverbs 23:13 *Withhold not correction from the child: for if thou beatest him with the rod, he shall not die. 14 Thou shalt beat him with the rod, and shalt deliver his soul from hell.*

This verse tells you something about proper spankings. They don't result in death, or even in injury. Listen carefully: *A proper spanking should never leave bruises, cuts, or any type of injuries.* There is a difference between spanking and abusing. Spankings of children should be on the bottom, or maybe the back of the hand for little ones. And they should sting like crazy, but they should never cause cuts, bruises, or other injuries.

The older a child gets, the harder an adult may have to swing, but the result should still be the same; they should sting like crazy, but they should never cause cuts, bruises, or other injuries.

I was in the tenth grade. My English teacher told our class for about the tenth time to be quiet. He finally told us that he was headed out on an errand, but that if any of us were caught talking, the entire class was getting a paddling. A few minutes later, we were back at it. Laughing, giggling, whispering, passing notes, and he came in and caught us. He told us to all line up in the hall, and get ready for our paddling. Like a tough guy, I smarted off and said, "Well I guess I'll head for the front of the line." Now, I should mention at this point that this man was not only the English teacher in our school, but also the softball coach.

When that paddle hit my rear, I thought my eyes had popped out of my head. I didn't even flinch. I stood up, walked the three feet around the corner into the class... and collapsed on the floor in agony.

197

A second later I heard my buddy Greg get his. He got up, walked the three feet into the class, and collapsed beside me. I have had a broken arm, and have been bitten by a copperhead, but I have never had any part of my body hurt as bad as my tail did right then. But you know what? When I checked the ol' tail out in the mirror that night, there wasn't a trace. No bruises, no cuts, no indentations of a boat paddle, nothing!

Yes, I know that kids will wail like banshees, and that they think that spanking is killing them.

Dana went in to give our kids a promised spanking the other night. When they went to bend over, they had big square rear ends. They had stuffed the skirts and pants with big ol' books. Real original. Sorry kids, the books have to go, and the spanking won't kill you.

Kids who are allowed to do their own thing, and don't get spankings, end up humiliating their parents.

Proverbs 29:15 *The rod and reproof give wisdom: but a child left to himself bringeth his mother to shame.*

There was a kid who grew up in California to a wealthy family. Mom and dad never spanked him, gave him whatever he wanted, let him do whatever he wanted, and patted themselves on the back for being such "enlightened parents." That kid, John Walker Lindh, went overseas and joined an Islamic terrorist group, and got caught trying to kill other Americans. He became known as the American Taliban. When the media asked his parents what went wrong, they were humiliated that their son had turned out like that! They should have seen it coming. The rod and reproof give wisdom: but a child left to himself bringeth his mother to shame.

If you really want to be embarrassed when your kids get older, don't spank them when they are younger. Let them do whatever they want, let them scream and throw tantrums, let them disrespect you and other adults, let them have their way at all times, and you will accomplish your goal of producing kids that will humiliate you when they get older.

I have dealt with teens and twenty-somethings in the history of this church who, based on their bratty, self-absorbed behavior, I can just about guarantee you were not spanked as kids, or at least were not spanked consistently. Their parents perpetually had to apologize for the kid's rotten behavior. They were always red-faced and humiliated by what their kids were doing. Some kids who have been spanked will turn out like that, but MOST kids who are not spanked will turn out like that.

Kids need to be spanked while there is still hope for them.

Proverbs 19:18 *Chasten thy son while there is hope, and let not thy soul spare for his crying.*

There comes a time when it is too late. There comes a time when parents have let their kids run wild for too long, and at that point, all the spankings in the world will not help. When you become parents, you need to understand that the first five years of a child's life are the most formative years for him or her. If you give proper spankings from crawling age up to about age five, the rest of the growing up years will be pretty hopeful. But if you wait around until that child is half grown up, and then decide to start spanking, good luck, you are going to need it!

It breaks my heart to say it, but parents, if your child is a teenager and has never been spanked, it is too late for you to start now. Their course is set, and you just better pray that God intervenes.

Some practical advice and considerations.

We have already covered the fact that spankings should *never* leave cuts, bruises, or other injuries. But there are a few other practical things to consider:

Be very discreet where you spank, and whom you discuss it with.

Proverbs 22:3 *A prudent man foreseeth the evil, and hideth himself: but the simple pass on, and are punished.*

Proverbs 27:12 *A prudent man foreseeth the evil, and hideth himself; but the simple pass on, and are punished.*

It used to be that if a child cut up in public, mom or dad could yank that kid up, and wail his tail, and people standing around would go "good for you!" But now, if you spank a kid in public, some liberal busybody is likely to call DSS and try to take your kids. Because of that, some spankings may need to be postponed until you can get out of sight. If it is bad enough, I would literally get up from the restaurant table, leave a meal sitting there, and go home to spank my child. A meal can be replaced, a chance to train a child cannot.

Be careful whose questions you answer, and what you say.

Teachers, doctors, and other people are being trained now to ask kids and parents how discipline happens in their family. If you answer "spankings," you are liable to end up in a legal battle. I wouldn't lie, but I also wouldn't give people information that they didn't need to have. We were in the hospital with a family a couple of years ago, and had a nurse asked about this. I asked her what it had to do with the diabetes that this kid was struggling with! She looked stunned. She stammered around for a minute, and then said, "We just have to ask it, it's on the form." If it were me that they asked, I would have told them one of our forms of discipline, the nose in the corner routine, but I would not have bothered to tell her about spankings. She had no need to know.

If you are a kid who still gets spankings, thank God for parents who love you. You may think that they are the meanest people in the world. The truth is, the meanest people in the world are the people that hate you so bad, they would rather you never get a spanking and turn out to be a thug.

You especially whose children are grown, and in no danger of being harassed by DSS (By the way, we have some good folks in our church who work in different departments of DSS, and they are good folks with good sense) but you especially whose children are grown, and in no danger of being harassed by DSS need to be vocal in your support of spankings. Lots of times, parents with young kids are

200

rightly afraid to speak up, for fear of being harassed. You don't have that fear, so speak up! Write letters to the paper, call radio shows, call government officials, help these younger parents out!

Parents, do remember that on occasion, the "rod" can take different forms. Learn your child (especially your teen ones) and be creative.

We counseled one family to reduce their daughter to Laura Ingles clothes for a while. Worked wonders!

On another occasion, we told a mom with children too big to effectively spank to tell her kid this: if you give me an ounce more trouble, we are going to become the best of friends. I am going to go everywhere with you. I will make arrangements to be in all of your classes in school, where I will sit right beside you. I will walk down the halls holding your hand. Every one of your friends will see you with "mommy" 24/7... REALLY worked wonders!

Roses are red, my backside is too, for I smarted off, though surely I knew,
That momma and daddy, they loved me so much, that they would not tolerate backtalk and such.
So now I am lying, all sprawled on the floor, while momma and daddy walk out of my door.
They told me that this hurts them much more than me, but I'll not believe it till my backside I see!
If it's not a' broken into pieces galore, then I'll be surprised when I'm up off this floor.

PART SEVENTEEN:
EVERYTHING YOU NEED TO SEE IS UNDER THE CEILING

S ome time back there was a big women's seminar held. A woman was speaking on all types of marriage related subjects. One subject she covered was that men, irritatingly, often seem much more like children than mates. She asked the crowd "How many of you really want to mother your husband?" One woman out of all those hundreds raised her hand. The leader was somewhat surprised, and said, "You really want to mother your husband?" The lady replied "Mother? I thought you said smother!"

This message marks an interesting point in the series of messages, and the book coming from it. As I preach it, it will be the first time that the series has gotten ahead of the building. We will (alas) be done with the series before we are done with the building.

In just a few weeks (or months?) we will begin doing something that I have never done; we will be installing the drop ceiling. I've already been doing some homework on it. Talk about a unique thing! Basically, we will be hanging wires from the roof purlins, attaching them to metal grids, going around the perimeter of each room with an L-grid that attaches to the wall, and creating a 2x2 pattern overhead into which we will place 2x2, fire rated, recessed ceiling tiles. This will, like most everything else in the building, be a whole lot of work. And for what? Not to keep the rain out, the roof does that. So why have a ceiling under a roof? Why not just do without it? One simple reason: if we have everything that is hanging from the roof purlins exposed, the HVAC units and ducts, the electrical conduit, the junction boxes, the unistrut, the disconnects, and on and on, let me tell you what would happen. Every single service, there would be people thinking, "I wonder where the pipe from that light goes? I'll just trace it down. There it is, and then it goes that way, then curves under that beam, down the back wall, out through the side. Cool." And then someone else would look up at the air units, and they would think the same thing every one who has seen it lately has thought and said: "Man, that things looks like a spaceship!" And then they would mentally start to hear "dun dun dun, da dun dun duh dun, DA DUN.... Space. The final frontier. These are the voyages of the starship Enterprise. Its three-year mission: to seek out strange new worlds and new civilizations. To boldly go where no man has gone before!"

Those ceiling tiles keep all of that from happening. *They keep people from getting distracted from the things that are really important.* And so often in a home, it isn't some huge thing that eventually undermines the home, it is distraction. So let's see if we can't install some spiritual ceiling tiles in this chapter, and help us all get our focus right. Let me make several simple statements for our main points in this chapter.

The enemy in the home is the devil, not the spouse.

1 Peter 5:8 *Be sober, be vigilant; because your adversary the devil, as a roaring lion, walketh about, seeking whom he may devour:*

May I remind you that the first attack in the first home was an attack by the devil? So often, people in the home act as if their spouse is the enemy! The devil is the enemy, focus on that. Even when your spouse is lazy, irritating, and irresponsible, he or she is still not the enemy!

Just having your spouse around is pretty good stuff. If you don't believe me, ask anyone who has lost a spouse to death.

There are obviously exceptions to this truth. A wife-beater, a child abuser, having that kind of person around is no blessing. But other than such things as these, having a spouse around, even one that you want to strangle from time to time, is a lot better than doing without a spouse.

1 Corinthians 15:26 *The last enemy that shall be destroyed is death.*

There are times when I am irritated by my wonderful bride. But whenever I think of what things would be like if I lost her to the enemy, death, I realize that I need her and want her and am blessed by having her around. Life with your spouse is good. Focus on that.

Building people is a lot more important than building careers, houses, or anything else.

Jesus was on earth for 33 plus years. Who can name for me a single structure that He built? What degree did He earn?

Those things (buildings, careers, etc.) aren't wrong, but there is something far more important to build:

Matthew 10:1 *And when he had called unto him his twelve disciples, he gave them power against unclean spirits, to cast them out, and to heal all manner of sickness and all manner of disease. 2 Now the names of the twelve apostles are these; The first, Simon, who is called Peter, and Andrew his brother; James the son of Zebedee, and John his brother; 3 Philip, and Bartholomew; Thomas, and Matthew the publican; James the son of Alphaeus, and Lebbaeus, whose surname was Thaddaeus; 4 Simon the Canaanite, and Judas Iscariot, who also betrayed him*

These are the men that turned the world upside down. These are the men whose ministry 2000 years ago led to our being saved today. Just think of where they were and what they were like when God found them.

Many times, people have all of their focus bent towards building things that are good (career, education) when the number one thing we should be concentrating on building in a family is the people in the family.

Friday, the dump truck ran out of gas. Caleb and I immediately got the can, and started walking; I knew there was a gas station about a half-mile up the road. After about a tenth of a mile, a guy stopped and picked us up.

On the way to the station, he said "I'm just going right up here to the concrete place. If you'll wait at the station, I'll come back and get you and take you back to the truck." I told him "thanks, but when I get this can filled up, I'll go ahead and start walking back, and if you happen to catch up with me, I'll ride." So we got the gas, and started walking. Caleb asked me, "Dad, why didn't we wait there for that guy to pick us up so we wouldn't have to walk?" I told him, "Son, always, always, always do everything you can do, and when you do, God will send more help when you need it." I then talked to him about people that are lazy, and won't work, and expect the government to hand them a check, and how the Bible said if a man will not work, neither shall he eat." Then I told him again, "So always remember: do absolutely everything you can do for yourself, and when God sees your efforts, He will send people to help when it's time." At that very moment, I heard a familiar sounding "honk." I turned around, and it was Dana! I don't think my son will soon forget that lesson.

Husbands, use praise and love and tenderness and confidence to build up your wives.

Parents, use training and nurturing and work and never miss an opportunity to build up your children. If you live in a little shack, but build two or three fine children, you are better off than if you had built Microsoft and the Biltmore house! Focus on building the people in your family.

In everything you do, seen or unseen, remember that this life is not "the end of judgment." The Judgment seat of Christ is coming, and it is to be our ultimate focus when it comes to what we do!

2 Corinthians 5:9 *Wherefore we labour, that, whether present or absent, we may be accepted of him.* **10** *For we must all appear before the judgment seat of Christ; that every one may receive the things done in his body, according to that he hath done, whether it be good or bad.* **11** *Knowing therefore the terror of the Lord, we persuade men; but we are made manifest unto God; and I trust also are made manifest in your consciences.*

If we go through our days focused on that, imagine how different we would be!

Are you really going to look at that marriage-destroying pornography when you remember the Judgment seat of Christ?

Are you really going to commit adultery when you remember the Judgment seat of Christ?

Are you really going to bite your mate's head off when you remember the Judgment seat of Christ?

Are you really going to drink that home-wrecking booze when you remember the Judgment seat of Christ?

Focus, focus, focus!

PART EIGHTEEN:
JUST TO MAKE IT NICE

The man and his wife, both age 60, were celebrating their fortieth anniversary. On that special day, a good fairy appeared and said, "You have both been so faithful and loyal to each other, I will grant you both one wish." The wife looked at her husband, and saw his good work ethic, his faithfulness, and said "I want to take a trip around the world with my dear husband" and Poof! They were on a luxury liner, sailing through the Mediterranean. The husband looked at his wife, and saw... her wrinkles, and her age spots, and her bifocals. Seeing a golden opportunity, he said, "I wish to be married to a woman thirty years younger than me" and Poof! He was 90.

This has been a lot of fun for me, and I trust for you. We've spent seventeen chapters together looking at a home in the context of how much building a home is like building a building. We started at the very foundation, and now we've arrived at the finish nails.

All of the big stuff is done. Once the suspended ceiling is hung, there is really nothing more structurally or mechanically or electrically left. What we are left with is painting, and carpet, and molding, and decorating. All of that will take a while, but none of it is "nuts and bolts" kind of stuff. In fact, we could actually use our building without painting any of the walls. We could use the building without carpet. We could use the building without a single piece of molding, and without any decorations.

So if we could use the building without any of those things, why will we still take the time to paint the walls and to lay the carpet and put up molding and decorate? Real simple, *Just To Make It Nice.*

In this book we have covered some pretty heavyweight things, like finances and dealing with adultery and communication skills and child discipline. There have been a lot of these things that have made us say "ouch" as often as they have made us say "amen." Hopefully, this last chapter will provide more amens than ouches.

Psalm 16:5 *The LORD is the portion of mine inheritance and of my cup: thou maintainest my lot.* **6** *The lines are fallen unto me in pleasant places; yea, I have a goodly heritage.*

In this verse, the psalmist spoke spiritually, alluding back to something that happened historically. When the children of Israel came into the land of Canaan, there were twelve landholding tribes. In order to divide the land between them, lots were used. In other words, everyone was in a bit of suspense as to what parts of the land they would receive, where their boundary lines would fall. All of the land was wonderful, but some of those tribes, when they received their lot, had to say "Man! The lines are fallen unto me in *pleasant* places." In other words, there were some things, rolling hills, lovely valleys, rippling creeks, that made their homes nice. They could build anywhere, even in a barren desert if necessary, but they had the blessing of having a *pleasant* home.

Have you ever noticed how often it is the little things that make a difference? My wife's office in the old building is also the church storage room and the music room and the place where the offerings are counted and the computer room and the copy room. As such, it is a disaster about 90% of the time, and there isn't much that we can do about it till we get into the new building and she gets an actual secretarial office.

But in that office, on the desk, is a cup full of coffee beans. I absolutely love walking into her office just to smell the air! I secretly suspect that when we get to heaven, God is going to get all of the coffee drinkers together and say, "You drank that awful stuff? It was just for smell!"

None of this will plumb the depths of theology. This chapter isn't about that. This is just to help put on the finishing touches, it is just to help make some things so nice, that everyone, husband, wife, kids, loves being a part of the family, loves living in the home, and looks back with fondness on it for the rest of their lives.

Let me give you a warning at this point. You may be tempted to think, now or sometime during this chapter, "This stuff just doesn't sound very deep or spiritual. Let me help you with that right off the bat. What makes Heaven Heaven? Christ. So even if Heaven had nothing special about it, it would still be Heaven, just because of Jesus, right? Of course. We know that, and God knows that. But now look at this:

Revelation 21:10 *And he carried me away in the spirit to a great and high mountain, and shewed me that great city, the holy Jerusalem, descending out of heaven from God.*

Here is one small part of Heaven being described, the New Jerusalem, where we the saints of God will live forever. Now we already know that just having Jesus there would make it Heaven, right? But now look at this:

Revelation 21:18a *And the building of the wall of it was of jasper...*

This city that we will live in has a wall made of Jasper, a beautiful sea green colored stone. We didn't have to have that for it to be Heaven. It is not something that is "necessary" to make it Heaven. So if it isn't "necessary," why did God do it? Just to make it nice for us.

Revelation 21:18b *...and the city was pure gold, like unto clear glass.*

This city that we will live in is made of pure gold, translucent like clear glass. We didn't have to have that for it to be Heaven. It is

211

not something that is "necessary" to make it Heaven. So if it isn't "necessary," why did God do it? Just to make it nice for us.

Revelation 21:19 *And the foundations of the wall of the city were garnished with all manner of precious stones. The first foundation was jasper; the second, sapphire; the third, a chalcedony; the fourth, an emerald; 20 The fifth, sardonyx; the sixth, sardius; the seventh, chrysolite; the eighth, beryl; the ninth, a topaz; the tenth, a chrysoprasus; the eleventh, a jacinth; the twelfth, an amethyst. 21 And the twelve gates were twelve pearls; every several gate was of one pearl:*

This city that we will live in has twelve foundations that are garnished with precious stones. Jasper - Sea Green, Sapphire - Dark Blue, Chalcedony - Bluish white, Emerald - deep green, Sardonyx - light red, Sardius - Blood red, Chrysolyte - Yellow, Beryl - Bluish green, Topaz - Greenish yellow, Chrysoprasus - Yellowish blue, Jacinth - cinnamon color, Amethyst - deep purple. How beautiful! But we didn't have to have that for it to be Heaven. It is not something that is "necessary" to make it Heaven. So if it isn't "necessary," why did God do it? Just to make it nice for us.

Revelation 21:21 *And the twelve gates were twelve pearls; every several gate was of one pearl...*

The city that we will live in has twelve gates, each one made from one giant pearl. They could have been aluminum cattle gates. We didn't have to have gates of pearl for it to be Heaven. It is not something that is "necessary" to make it Heaven. So if it isn't "necessary," why did God do it? Just to make it nice for us.

Revelation 21:21b *...and the street of the city was pure gold, as it were transparent glass.*

In this city that we will live in, Main Street is purest gold! Asphalt would have done fine. We didn't have to have a golden street for it to be Heaven. It is not something that is "necessary" to make it Heaven. So if it isn't "necessary," why did God do it? Just to make it nice for us.

Revelation 22:1 *And he shewed me a pure river of water of life, clear as crystal, proceeding out of the throne of God and of the Lamb.* (Was that necessary? No.) *2 In the midst of the street of it, and on either side of the river, was there the tree of life, which bare twelve manner of fruits, and yielded her fruit every month: and the leaves of the tree were for the healing of the nations* (Was that necessary? No.)

Once again, these little touches are just to make it nice for us.

God loves us so much that He takes extra special care just to make things nice for us. So as we go through this message, please remember that when we take care to do the little things that make it nice for our families, we are just doing for our families what Christ does for us! And I promise you, if you actually care enough to do the little extras for your family, your family will stand a much greater chance of surviving, and even thriving.

As I go through this list, I expect your minds to wander a bit from time to time, and in this case it will be a good thing, because you will doubtless think of some things that I haven't thought of. So write down my list, add your own ideas to the list, and if you have any real good ideas that I've missed, tell me about them so you can help me as much as I hope to help you.

Family traditions help to make it nice.

On Sunday mornings, we head for BoJangles. We have been doing this for years. There are other places out there, but this is just a family tradition for us. We go through the drive through, and get two medium Cajun Fillet Biscuit combos with seasoned fries and diet Pepsi, two egg biscuits, and one egg and cheese biscuit. Just writing it makes me hungry.

At Christmas, dinner and gifts are at the Sessions house on Christmas Eve, and then it has always been on to my grandmother's house on Christmas day. All the gifts are piled at random around the tree. When it comes gift time, it is pandemonium as Chip picks up a gift, finds the name, and then goes for the next one.

Last year, a newer member of the family organized the gifts into piles by name. When we walked in, and saw all that nice, neat, tidiness, and realized that there would not be the excitement of wondering whom the next gift was for, I nearly went nutty. I looked over at Stephanie, and she was as perplexed as I was. You just don't go messing with tradition like that!

When I was growing up, all during the months of November and December, there was eggnog in the fridge. Now that is true in my home as well.

The demolition derby is a tradition for us. "Wild Wanda" won the women's division this year. She crawled out on to the top of the car, and started jumping up and down on it. When she was done, it looked like it had been stomped by Sasquatch. The crowd went wild!

Caleb and I go on the Ferris wheel at the fair every year. Four years in a row now.

Dana and I have watched the Muppet's Christmas Carol on Christmas Eve – 13 years in a row as of the writing of this book. I could quote it by heart.

Are these things "deeply spiritual?" No more so than the wall of Jasper. *They are just to make it nice.*

Good smells help to make it nice

Did you know that even God likes things that smell good?

Exodus 29:25 *And thou shalt receive them of their hands, and burn them upon the altar for a burnt offering, for a sweet savour* (a sweet smell, fragrance, aroma) *before the LORD: it is an offering made by fire unto the LORD.*

Forty times in the Bible we read about something smelling nice to God. Sometimes it was in the spiritual sense, like II Corinthians 2:15, but the overwhelming majority of those forty times were when people put a literal sacrifice on a literal altar and it literally smelled sweet to God.

Throughout the books of the law, God gave recipes for sweet smelling incense of the apothecary:

Exodus 30:35 *And thou shalt make it a perfume, a confection after the art of the apothecary, tempered together, pure and holy:*

God gave the recipe for this. God likes things that smell sweet.

He made us in is image. Sweet smells help to make our home nice:

Fresh baked cookies

Yankee Candles (Storm watch is my wife's favorite. I like cinnamon apple, and raspberry spice.)

Coffee

Potpourri

When we have an apple that has gotten too soft to eat, Dana puts it in a pot of water with cinnamon and cloves on the stove, and let's it simmer on the stove. Awesome!

Lemon or orange based cleaners (raw Clorox will do the job, but ewwwwww. Who wants the house to smell like a hospital?)

Are these nice smells deeply spiritual? No, they're kind of like the street of gold; they just help to make it nice.

Family meals help to make it nice

Luke 22:15 *And he said unto them, With desire I have desired to eat this passover with you before I suffer:*

For all practical purposes, the disciples were about the only family Jesus really had on earth. And here He is, shortly before His death, indicating how glad He is that He can sit down and eat one more Passover meal with them.

In Revelation 2:17, we find that Christ Himself will serve us a special meal in Heaven:

Revelation 2:17b ... *To him that overcometh will I give to eat of the hidden manna...*

When we get to heaven, there will be a big family meal waiting for us:

Revelation 19:9 a *And he saith unto me, Write, Blessed are they which are called unto the marriage supper of the Lamb...*

It is good in heaven, and it is good on earth. But unfortunately, this is going away in our fast-paced culture, and it is a shame. Find a way to have family meals!

Growing up, Sunday afternoon was our day for this. We often had four generations around the table together.

My grandma made a gumbo to die for. My aunt made a crock-pot mac and cheese. My Grandfather broke out the crackers and the port-wine cheese. Unforgettable.

Whenever the Sessions are home, we try and eat with them, even if it means eating out. Meal times are great times for fellowship with families.

When Dana and I got married, we started going down to Alabama over Thanksgiving for the big meal with her family. I got to know all of them through that.

Find time, regularly, to eat together as a family. Is it deeply spiritual? No, it is kind of like the gates of pearl, it is just to make it nice.

Outings and vacations help to make it nice

Mark 6:31 *And he said unto them, Come ye yourselves apart into a desert place, and rest a while: for there were many coming and going, and they had no leisure so much as to eat.*

I am glad to know that the Master expects us not just to rest, but even to get away and rest for a while. When you take outings and vacations, you are obeying the very words of Christ.

I preached this while I was still in Bible College, and had a group of geeky little twerps chew me out over it. They didn't think it was right to take vacations and outings when people were dying and going to hell. Well, they went their way, disobeying the words of Christ, I went my way, obeying the words of Christ, and all these years later, I am the only one out of that argument still in the ministry. Lots of those guys not only have lost their ministry, but their families as well. God knows what He is talking about.

Outings and vacations help to make things nice in a family!

We take our vacation with the Sessions every year. It is great family fellowship. And how spiritual a giant must I be, to have my mother-in-law along for vacation every year? (Love ya, Mom!)

Trips to the zoo. Going camping. Driving up in to the mountains to see the leaves. This stuff doesn't even have to cost much at all, but family outings and vacations do help to build life-long bonds within your family.

Are they deeply spiritual? No, they're like the River of Life; they're just to make it nice.

Game times help to make it nice

Man, growing up, we had some awesome game times. I remember some world-class monopoly games. I know the Keeners are monopoly people. The kids call Dave "The Mo Daddy."

The Conyers are Cranium people.

My grandfather was a chess man. He was the chess champ at Tulane University. I will never forget finally beating him. One of the highlights of my life.

Caleb and I duel at checkers and tic-tac-toe.

I used to play my wife at Othello. Not anymore. Only a fool volunteers to get humiliated repeatedly!

Throw a ball. Toss a frisbee. Play hide and seek, do something! It's not that playing games is deeply Spiritual, it's just that they're kind of like the Tree of Life; they're just there to make it nice.

Generational ties help to make it nice

Job 42:16 *After this lived Job an hundred and forty years, and saw his sons, and his sons' sons, even four generations. 17 So Job died, being old and full of days.*

Job didn't just *have* sons and grandsons and great grandsons, and great-great grandsons; he *saw* his sons and grandsons and great grandsons, and great- great grandsons. He had contact with them.

Do you know one of the things I like best about my wife? Her parents. Do you know one of the things the Sessions like best about me? My kids. My kids love both their parents and their grandparents. We have three generations with very close ties.

You know what? You can have a family unit of just you and your wife, no kids, and no contact with either of your parents. You can do that. But it's not near as nice as intentionally having multi-generational ties.

Even if the grandparents or great grandparents are in a nursing home somewhere, keep those ties strong. Visit often, bring pictures.

And go beyond that. Teach your kids about the relatives that died before they were born. It gives a good feeling when you see yourself as part of a family that has come from across the world, through the centuries.

These generational ties, are they deeply spiritual? No, they serve the same purpose as the mansions John 14 speaks about; they're just to make it nice.

A woman's touch in decorating helps to make it nice

There is a word for a man who talks funny and can out-decorate any woman. That word is *GAY.* Men, if your wife patches the hole in the roof while you arrange the flowers on the table, don't walk behind me.

I have no desire to match drapes and furniture fabric, or arrange the flowers, or pick out just the right wallpaper. But I sure enjoy living in a house where my wife does all those things!

Ma'am, you may not think of yourself as much of a decorator, and compared to other ladies, you may not be. But compared to your husband, you are probably Martha Stewart.

A roof, a floor, and four walls isn't a home, it is a cell. A roof a floor four walls and a woman's touch decorating it all up, that is a home, a nice one.

You don't have to shop at Belks and spend thousands. I know a family down in Alabama that decorated their entire house with stuff they got from yard sales and antique shops, and man it is nice!

This decorating stuff isn't deeply spiritual. It's like that green rainbow around the throne, it's just to make it nice.

Selective silliness helps to make it nice
Proverbs 17:22 *A merry heart doeth good like a medicine: but a broken spirit drieth the bones.*

My grandfather, a certified genius, stern as he was, would often break into a song: "Lazy bones, sleeping in the sun, how you 'spect to get your days work done? Never get your days work done, sleeping in the evening sun..."

I am a big believer in, and strong practitioner of, selective silliness. From early in their lives, when my kids would ask me where we were going to eat, I would quote them this little ditty that I made up on the spot:

The bug barn! Big juicy bugs and grimy slimy worms and crunchy wunchy crickets Mmm mm!
Other times, I would sing them this song:

Oh I love my little knot heads, little knot heads, little knot heads, oh I love my little knot heads, my three little knot heads. There's Caleb knot and Karis knot and Aléthia knot, they've knots a lot, oh I love my little knot heads, my three little knot heads.

Man, some of the guys I went to Bible College with would have a stroke over hearing this. But you know what? Probably twenty times a day my kids run up to me for no reason at all, hug me, kiss me on the cheek, and say "I love you daddy." But a lot of the "serious Solomon's" don't even get to see their kids anymore except with supervised visitation. Mom, Dad, if you are all serious all the time, your home may well survive, but it won't be very enjoyable.

Selective silliness isn't deeply spiritual. It's like the sea of glass in Heaven that we read about in Revelation chapters four and fifteen; it's just to make things nice.

219

Enjoying the seasons helps to make it nice

Look what God said right after the flood:

Genesis 8:22 *While the earth remaineth, seedtime and harvest, and cold and heat, and summer and winter, and day and night shall not cease.*

God made all four seasons. There is something nice about all four seasons. Enjoy whatever it is about them that make them nice:

In the springtime watch the flowers bloom, take walks, swing on the porch swing, fly a kite.

In the summer, grill out, jump in the river, go rafting.

In the fall, sleep with the windows open when it gets cool at night, fish, hunt, watch the leaves turn, make pumpkin pie.

In the winter, make hot chocolate, walk in the snow, have snowball fights, breath out just to watch your breath vaporize.

God made the seasons for you to enjoy. Do it!

Are these seasonal pleasures deeply spiritual? No, they are like the crowns we will earn and then cast at His feet; they're just to make it nice.

When you read the first chapter of the book of Genesis, the account of God creating our world, you find that the very first adjective ever used in the Bible is the word *good.* That word occurs seven times to describe what God made for us. That English word *good* is from the Hebrew word *towb.* It means good in the sense of *pleasant and agreeable.* In the very first chapter of the Bible, God was doing things just to make it nice. In the very last chapter of the Bible, God was doing things just to make it nice for us.

In your own home that God has been so kind to give you, don't stop with the footers. Go all the way to the finish nails. Do all of the little things that will make your family say, "Wow, I really enjoy being a part of this family."

God bless you, and your family!

ENDNOTES

[1]Jonathan Edwards and Ellyn Sanna, *Religious Affections*, (Uhrichsville, OH; Barbour Publishing, Inc., 1999) 12-13

[2]Arnold Dallimore, [http://www.sermonillustrations.com]

[3]Today in the Word, MBI, December, 1989, p. 20, Swindoll, You and Your Problems Transformed by Thorns, p. 58.

[4][http://www.sermonillustrations.com]

EPILOGUE

As I finish this book, I am pleased to report that we are now in our new building. I am sitting at my desk, looking around at a 14-foot ceiling, a couch, new bookshelves, and pretty blue carpet. After eleven years in a little dungeon with seven-foot high ceilings, a room that also doubled as a Sunday school class, I now have a real office! My wife is next door in her new office. We have been in the building for about three months now, and it means so very much to us, since we did it all ourselves. The project took us two and a half years from start to finish. God was, and continues to be, so very good to us. If you are ever nearby, come and be with us for service! Pray for us, for we desire to see God strengthen homes through the ministry He has given us. I pray that this book may play a vital part in that mission.

Dr. Bo Wagner

Made in the USA
Charleston, SC
26 May 2011